WORD 2000
FOR WINDOWS®
FOR
DUMMIES®

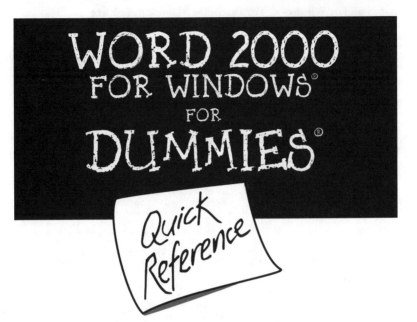

Quick Reference

by Peter Weverka

Hungry Minds™

HUNGRY MINDS, INC.

New York, NY ◆ Cleveland, OH ◆ Indianapolis, IN

Chicago, IL ◆ Foster City, CA ◆ San Francisco, CA

Word 2000 For Windows® For Dummies® Quick Reference

Published by
Hungry Minds, Inc.
909 Third Avenue
New York, NY 10022
www.hungryminds.com

Library of Congress Catalog Card No.: 99-60928

ISBN: 0-7645-0449-5

Printed in the United States of America

10 9 8 7 6 5 4

1O/SX/QS/QR/IN

Distributed in the United States by Hungry Minds, Inc.

Distributed by CDG Books Canada Inc. for Canada; by Transworld Publishers Limited in the United Kingdom; by IDG Norge Books for Norway; by IDG Sweden Books for Sweden; by IDG Books Australia Publishing Corporation Pty. Ltd. for Australia and New Zealand; by TransQuest Publishers Pte Ltd. for Singapore, Malaysia, Thailand, Indonesia, and Hong Kong; by Gotop Information Inc. for Taiwan; by ICG Muse, Inc. for Japan; by Intersoft for South Africa; by Eyrolles for France; by International Thomson Publishing for Germany, Austria and Switzerland; by Distribuidora Cuspide for Argentina; by LR International for Brazil; by Galileo Libros for Chile; by Ediciones ZETA S.C.R. Ltda. for Peru; by WS Computer Publishing Corporation, Inc., for the Philippines; by Contemporanea de Ediciones for Venezuela; by Express Computer Distributors for the Caribbean and West Indies; by Micronesia Media Distributor, Inc. for Micronesia; by Chips Computadoras S.A. de C.V. for Mexico; by Editorial Norma de Panama S.A. for Panama; by American Bookshops for Finland.

For general information on Hungry Minds' products and services please contact our Customer Care Department within the U.S. at 800-762-2974, outside the U.S. at 317-572-3993 or fax 317-572-4002.

For sales inquiries and reseller information, including discounts, premium and bulk quantity sales, and foreign-language translations, please contact our Customer Care Department at 800-434-3422, fax 317-572-4002, or write to Hungry Minds, Inc., Attn: Customer Care Department, 10475 Crosspoint Boulevard, Indianapolis, IN 46256.

For information on licensing foreign or domestic rights, please contact our Sub-Rights Customer Care Department at 650-653-7098.

For information on using Hungry Minds' products and services in the classroom or for ordering examination copies, please contact our Educational Sales Department at 800-434-2086 or fax 317-572-4005.

Please contact our Public Relations Department at 212-884-5163 for press review copies or 212-884-5000 for author interviews and other publicity information or fax 212-884-5400.

For authorization to photocopy items for corporate, personal, or educational use, please contact Copyright Clearance Center, 222 Rosewood Drive, Danvers, MA 01923, or fax 978-750-4470.

About the Author

Peter Weverka is the author of 17 computer books, including *Dummies 101: Microsoft Office 2000 For Windows* and *Money 99 For Dummies,* both published by IDG Books Worldwide, Inc. His humorous articles and stories (none related to computers, thankfully) have appeared in *Harper's* and *SPY* magazine.

Peter is also an editor. He has polished, cleaned up, and actually read over 80 computer books on topics ranging from word processing to desktop publishing to the Internet. He edited about 50 of those books online with Microsoft Word.

Peter believes that the goal of all computing is to help you get your work done faster so you don't have to sit in front of the computer anymore. His favorite pastime is pruning trees; his greatest pleasure, jawing with his children.

Dedication

For Ethel and Bob.

Author's Acknowledgments

This book owes a lot to many different people. I would especially like to thank project editor Andrea Boucher, who kept everything on track and saw this book through to completion, and this book's copy editors, Tina Sims and Kathleen Dobie, who wielded the editorial scalpel so skillfully.

Thanks as well go to technical editor Jim McCarter, who did a superb job of making sure that every task in this book is indeed explained correctly, and to Richard Evans, who wrote the index.

I would be remiss if I didn't thank the editors who helped me with the two previous editions of this book: Bill Helling, Pam Mourouzis, Michael Simsic, Gareth Hancock, and Meg Bonar.

I also owe a debt to these people at IDG Books who worked so hard on my book: Tom Missler, Linda Boyer, Chrissie Johnson, Jacque Schneider, Janet Seib, Christine Berman, Kelli Botta, Jennifer Mahern, Ethel M. Winslow, Janet M. Withers, and the whole production team.

Finally, my heartfelt thanks go to my family — Sofia, Henry, and Addie — who were most indulgent of my odd working hours and my strange, vampirelike demeanor in the morning.

Peter Weverka
San Francisco
January 1999

Publisher's Acknowledgments

We're proud of this book; please send us your comments through our Hungry Minds Online Registration Form located at: www.dummies.com.

Some of the people who helped bring this book to market include the following:

Acquisitions, Editorial, and Media Development

Project Editor: Andrea C. Boucher
(Previous Edition: Bill Helling)

Acquisitions Editor: Steven H. Hayes

Copy Editors: Tina Sims, Kathleen Dobie

Technical Editor: Jim McCarter

Editorial Manager: Kelly Ewing

Media Development Manager: Heather Heath Dismore

Editorial Assistant: Paul E. Kuzmic

Production

Project Coordinator: Tom Missler

Layout and Graphics: Linda M. Boyer, J. Tyler Connor, Angela F. Hunckler, Chrissie Johnson, Brent Savage, Jacque Schneider, Janet Seib

Proofreaders: Christine Berman, Kelli Botta, Sarah Fraser, Jennifer Mahern, Ethel M. Winslow, Janet M. Withers

Indexer: Infodex Indexing Services, Inc.

General and Administrative

Hungry Minds, Inc.: John Kilcullen, CEO; Bill Barry, President and COO; John Ball, Executive VP, Operations & Administration; John Harris, CFO

Hungry Minds Technology Publishing Group: Richard Swadley, Senior Vice President and Publisher; Mary Bednarek, Vice President and Publisher, Networking and Certification; Walter R. Bruce III, Vice President and Publisher, General User and Design Professional; Joseph Wikert, Vice President and Publisher, Programming; Mary C. Corder, Editorial Director, Branded Technology Editorial; Andy Cummings, Publishing Director, General User and Design Professional; Barry Pruett, Publishing Director, Visual

Hungry Minds Manufacturing: Ivor Parker, Vice President, Manufacturing

Hungry Minds Marketing: John Helmus, Assistant Vice President, Director of Marketing

Hungry Minds Online Management: Brenda McLaughlin, Executive Vice President, Chief Internet Officer

Hungry Minds Production for Branded Press: Debbie Stailey, Production Director

Hungry Minds Sales: Roland Elgey, Senior Vice President, Sales and Marketing; Michael Violano, Vice President, International Sales and Sub Rights

♦

The publisher would like to give special thanks to Patrick J. McGovern, without whom this book would not have been possible.

♦

Contents at a Glance

Table of Contents

Part III: Formatting Documents and Text 55

How to Use This Book

Keep this book on the corner of your desk. When you want to try something new, want to try something you're unsure of, or tell yourself that *there has to be a better way,* open this book, and I'll tell you what it is and how to do it.

This little book cannot cover every nook and cranny of Microsoft Word 2000, but it covers the fundamental things that everybody needs to know. And it gives you enough instruction so that you can get going on the complicated things.

Over the years, I've discovered a lot of shortcuts and tricks for using this program. I've thrown them into the mix, too, so that you can be the beneficiary of my many years of blind groping and daring experimentation.

What's in This Book, Anyway?

To find what you're looking for in this book, your best bet is to go to the index and table of contents. Other than that, I've organized this book into eight parts, and you are invited to browse in one part or another until you find what you are looking for.

◆ Part I describes basic techniques and translates ugly word-processing jargon into modern American English.

◆ Part II explains the editing tasks that everyone who wants to use this program wisely should know. You'll find a lot of shortcuts in Part II.

◆ Part III describes formatting. A document communicates by its words but also by the way it is laid out. In Part III, I tell you how to format a document so that readers know what's what just by glancing at the page.

◆ In Part IV, I explain printing. When you can't print things correctly, it's a nightmare. I hope you never have to visit Part IV.

◆ Part V tells you how to make your work go faster. If you're going to browse, browse in Part V. You'll discover things that you wouldn't think to look for on your own.

◆ Part VI sort of picks up where Part III left off. In many ways, Word 2000 is more of a desktop publishing program than a word processing program. Part VI looks at Word's desktop publishing features and also explains how to create Web pages and a Web site with Word.

◆ Part VII delves into the fancy and the esoteric. It explains cross-references, footnotes, tables of contents, and other things of use to people who create complex documents.

◆ Part VIII is a hodgepodge conglomeration of the strange and useful. It explains how to back up documents, find missing files, and see how many minutes you've worked on a document, among other things.

◆ At the end of this book is a short glossary of computer terms. If you need to know what *cursor, field, cell,* and other peculiar terms mean, have a look in the glossary.

The Cast of Icons

To help you get more out of this book, I place icons here and there. Here's what the icons mean:

Microsoft Weird 2000 has a few odd features and quirks. You can't spell words certain ways without being "AutoCorrected," for example. Try entering a lowercase letter after a period — you can't do it. Word does weird things because it makes a lot of assumptions about what the typical user wants. You, however, may not be a typical user. When I describe the weird things that Word does, I put a Weirdness icon in the margin.

Of course, Word has a lot of great stuff, too. I'm sure you know that, or else you wouldn't be using Word. Where I describe how to use Word's speedy, wonderful, advantageous, effective, and powerful features (I'm getting these adjectives from a thesaurus), I put a Cool Stuff icon in the margin.

Next to the Tip icon, you find shortcuts and tricks of the trade.

Where you see this icon, tread softly and carefully. It means that you are opening Pandora's box or doing something that you may regret later.

In Word, there are usually two ways to do everything — the fast but dicey way and the slow but thorough way. When I explain how to do a task the fast way, I put a Fast Track icon in the margin.

If you need more information than this book provides, look for these icons. They tell you which topics are covered in more detail in other *...For Dummies* (IDG Books Worldwide, Inc.) books. This icon also refers you to other parts of *this* book for more information on a given topic.

Conventions Used in This Book

To help you figure things out quickly and get the most out of this book, I've adopted a few conventions.

Where I tell you to click a button, a picture of the button appears in the left-hand margin. For example, the button you see here is the Save button. Where I tell you to "click the Save button to save your document," you see the Save button to the left so that you know exactly which button to click.

Besides clicking buttons, you can do tasks in Word by pressing combinations of keys. For example, you can save a document by pressing Ctrl+S. In other words, you can press the Ctrl key and the S key at the same time. Where you see Ctrl+, Alt+, or Shift+ and a key name (or maybe more than one key name), press the keys simultaneously.

To show how to issue commands, I use the ⇨ symbol. For example, you can choose File⇨Save to save a document. The ⇨ is just a shorthand method of saying, "Choose Save from the File menu."

Notice how the *F* in *File* and the *S* in *Save* are underlined in the preceding paragraph. Those same characters are underlined in the command names in Word. Underlined letters are called *hot keys*. You can press them to give commands and make selections in dialog boxes. Where a letter is underlined in a command name or on a dialog box in Word, it is also underlined on the pages of this book.

Step-by-step directions in this book are numbered to make directions easier to follow. When you're doing a task, do it by the numbers. Sometimes, however, you have to make choices in order to give a command. When you have to make a choice in a dialog box or you have different options for completing a task, I present the choices in a bulleted list. For example, here are the three ways to save a document:

+ Choose File⇨Save

+ Press Ctrl+S

+ Click the Save button

Where you see letters in boldface text in this book, it means to type the letters. For example, if you read "Type **annual report** in the File Name text box to name your document," you should do just that. You should type those very same letters.

Finally, a word about how option names are capitalized in Word dialog boxes. In the dialog boxes, many option names are shown in lowercase except for the first letter. For example, in the Print dialog box is an option called Number of copies. In this book, however, that scroll box is called Number of Copies, with a capital *C* in *copies*. I capitalize the first letter to make it easier for you to read option names in this book. Therefore, don't worry if the option names in this book are a little different from the ones in the Word dialog boxes.

I'd Like to Hear from You

Best of luck to you. Every trick I know of for getting the most out of Word 2000 is in this book. If you've discovered a trick of your own and would like to share it with me, I would be most grateful. And if you have a question about using Word, send it to me. I will answer it as soon as I can, notwithstanding my busy schedule. Please e-mail comments and questions to me at Peter_Weverka@msn.com.

Part 1

Getting to Know Word 2000

If you've been around word processors for a while, you needn't read this part of the book. But if you haven't used a word processor before, read on. I tell you what mysterious words like *cursor, double-click,* and *scroll* mean. I give you the basics so that you can get going with Word 2000.

In this part . . .

- ✓ What a document is, exactly
- ✓ What the pointer, cursor, and the other weird stuff on-screen are
- ✓ Finding your way around the keyboard
- ✓ Making menu choices and filling in a dialog box
- ✓ What the different parts of the screen are
- ✓ Starting Word 2000

What Is a Document?

Document is just a fancy word for a letter, report, announcement, or proclamation that you create with Word.

When you first start Word, you see a document with the generic name "Document1." But if you already have a document on-screen and you want to start a new one, click the New Blank Document button. A brand-new document opens with the generic name "Document2" in the title bar. (The *title bar* is the stripe across the top of the computer screen.) It's called "Document2" because it's the second one you're working on. The document keeps that name, Document2, until you save it and give it a name of your own.

Cursors and Pointers

Cursors and *pointers* are little symbols that let you know where you are on-screen and what the computer is doing. There are a bunch of different cursors and pointers, but the only ones you really need to know about are listed in the following table:

Cursor/Pointer		What It Does
I	Insertion point	Sits in the text and blinks on and off. All the action takes place at the insertion point: When you start typing, text appears at this point, and when you paste something from the Clipboard, it appears at the insertion point.
↖	Mouse cursor	Moves around on-screen when you move your mouse. Jiggle your mouse to see what the mouse cursor is. When this cursor is over something that you can select — a menu item or a button, for example — it turns into an arrow. Click the mouse when it's an arrow to select a menu item or press a button. When the mouse cursor is over text, it looks like a large, egotistical *I*. To enter text in a new place, move the *I*, click, and start typing.
⧗	Busy cursor	When Word is very busy, you see an hourglass on-screen. Twiddle your thumbs until the hourglass disappears and you can get back to work.
👆	Link Select cursor	When you move the pointer over a hyperlink, you see the Link Select cursor, a gloved hand. A *hyperlink* is a link between two documents or a document and a page on the Internet. Click a hyperlink and you travel to another document or a Web page.

The Keyboard

Most of the keys on the keyboard are familiar to you, but what about those weird keys camping out on the edges? Start in the upper-left corner of the keyboard and proceed clockwise:

Key (s)	What It Does
Esc	Backs you out of whatever you're doing. If you pull down a menu or open a dialog box and are frightened by what you see, you can always press Esc to get out.
F1– F12	These are the *function keys*. You press them alone or in combination with the Ctrl and Shift keys to get various things done quickly.
Print Scrn	Press this key to take a picture of your computer screen. The picture is copied to the Clipboard. From there, you can paste it into Word documents.
Scroll Lock, Pause	These keys are like the human appendix. They were good for something in the computer's evolutionary past, but now they just take up space on the keyboard.
~	The tilde key is the easiest key to overlook, but you sometimes need to press this key to enter Web site addresses.
	Press the Backspace key to erase letters to the left of the insertion point.
Insert	In most word processing applications, you press this key when you want the letters you type to cover the letters that are already there. Not so in Word. To "overtype" words and letters, double-click OVR on the status bar along the bottom of the screen.
Home	Pressing Home moves the insertion point to the left margin. A second Home key, which does the same thing as the first Home key, appears on the numeric keypad, where it rooms with the number 7.
Page Up	Press this key to move the insertion point up one computer-screen length in the document. You also find this key on the numeric keypad, along with the number 9, where it has the hiccuppy name PgUp.
Enter	A very important key. Press it to end a paragraph in Word or to say "okay" to the settings in a dialog box.
Delete	Press this key to remove characters to the right of the insertion point. You can also select sentences, paragraphs, or even whole pages and press Delete to remove gobs of text in one mighty blow. On the numeric keypad, this key is called Del.

(continued)

WARNING

Key (s)	What It Does
End	Moves the insertion point to the end of a line of text. You can also find it on the numeric keypad, where it shares space with the number 1.
Page Down	Moves the insertion point downward in a document by the length of one computer screen. This key also appears on the numeric keypad, where you find it along with the number 3.
Num Lock	Press Num Lock to make the keys on the numeric keypad act like number keys instead of direction keys. If you see numbers on-screen when you want to move the insertion point instead, Num Lock is on when it shouldn't be. Press Num Lock again to make the keys on the numeric keypad act like direction keys.
← ↑ → and ↓	These *arrow keys,* which share space on the numeric keypad with the 4, 8, 6, and 2, respectively, move the insertion point left, up, right, and down on-screen. You find another set of arrow keys at the bottom of the keyboard, between the numeric keypad and the Ctrl key.
Ctrl	The Control key. Press this one along with function keys and letter keys to make Word work quickly. For example, the fastest way to save a document is to press Ctrl+S. The keyboard boasts two Ctrl keys, one each below the Shift keys.
Alt	The Alternate key. Like Ctrl, this is another cattle prod to get Word to do things quickly. Press Alt and one of the underlined letters on the menu bar to pull down a menu when you're in a hurry.
Shift	Press this key and a letter to get a capital letter instead of a measly lowercase one.
Caps Lock	Someday soon, you'll be typing along AND DARNIT, YOU START GETTING ALL CAPITAL LETTERS. That's because you accidentally pressed the Caps Lock key. Press it again to go back to lowercase, or press it when you *want* to type ALL UPPERCASE letters.

Giving Commands

To give commands in Word, you can click a button, press a shortcut key combination, or choose an option from a menu. Get to know all the ways to give commands and you will be promoted from private to commander in chief.

Giving commands from menus

One way to give commands is to start from the menu bar. The *menu bar* is the list of menus near the top of the screen:

To *pull down* a menu from this list, you can either click the menu name with the mouse or press the Alt key and the underlined letter in the menu name. For example, to pull down the <u>E</u>dit menu, you can either click the word Edit or press Alt+E. When you do either, a *menu* appears as if by magic.

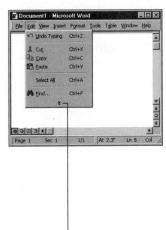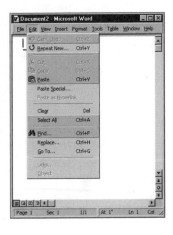

Click to see more commands

Now you have several *menu commands* to choose from. Sometimes, however, not all the commands on a menu appear. To make menus less confusing, all but the most common commands don't start appearing on a menu until you choose them for the first time. If you want to see all the commands a menu offers, click the double arrows at the bottom of the menu or simply leave the mouse pointer on the menu for a second or two.

Suppose that you want to choose the <u>F</u>ind command on the Edit menu. After the Edit menu drops down, you can either click the word Find or press the letter *F* on your keyboard to start searching.

Notice that some menu commands have *ellipses* (three dots) next to their names. When you choose one of these menu commands, a dialog box appears on-screen. ***See also*** "Filling In a Dialog Box" a bit further ahead if you need to know about dialog boxes.

Clicking a command with an arrow next to its name gives you a *submenu* — a short menu with more commands to choose from.

Shortcut keys for doing it quickly

Next to some commands on menus are Ctrl+key combinations called *shortcut keys.* If you want to select all the text in a document, for example, you can just press Ctrl+A, the shortcut key equivalent of the Select All command on the Edit menu.

Lots of menu commands have shortcut keys that help you get your work done faster. If you find yourself using a command often, see whether it has a shortcut key and start using the shortcut key to save time. Many commands have buttons next to their names as well. Instead of choosing these commands from menus, you can simply click a button on a toolbar.

Those mysterious shortcut menus

Shortcut menus are mysterious little menus that sometimes pop up when you click the right mouse button. For example, if you click the right mouse button in the middle of a document, you see a shortcut menu with basic editing commands. Or try right-clicking a word with a squiggly red line underneath it. You see a shortcut menu with suggestions for correcting a misspelled word:

squiggley

Filling In a Dialog Box

When Word needs a lot of information to complete a command, a *dialog box* appears on-screen. You have to fill out the dialog box before Word will do what you ask it to do. For example, when you ask Word to print a document, you get this dialog box:

Drop-down lists   Scroll list

Radio buttons   Check boxes

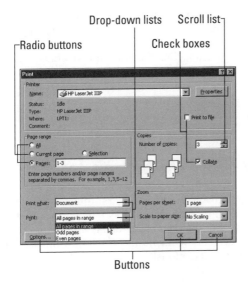

Buttons

At the bottom are two *drop-down lists*. Click the down-pointing arrow and down comes a list of options you can choose from.

Notice the Number of Copies *scroll list* in the Print dialog box. Click the little arrow that points up and the number climbs so that you can print two, three, four, or more copies. Click the little down-pointing arrow to get back to three, two, and one copy.

Four *radio buttons* tell Word which part of the document to print. The thing to know about radio buttons is that you can choose only one, just like you can listen to "Super Country KCOW" *or* to "Rockin' KROQ," but not both radio stations at once. In this dialog box, the radio buttons let you choose whether you print the whole document, the page the cursor is in, a selection of text, or a range of pages.

At the bottom of the Print dialog box are some buttons. Most dialog boxes have an OK and a Cancel button. Click OK (or press the Enter key) after you fill out the dialog box and you're ready for Word to execute the command. Click Cancel if you lose your nerve and want to start all over again.

Notice the two *check boxes* in the Print dialog box. You can click both check boxes, either check box, or neither check box. Check boxes work like radio buttons, except that you can select more than one, or none at all.

Some dialog boxes offer *tabs* that you can click to see more options. For example, the Options dialog box (choose Tools⇨ Options) has a grand total of ten tabs. If you want to change how Word saves documents, click the Save tab. To change the view settings, click the View tab, and so on.

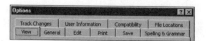

What All That Stuff On-Screen Is

Seeing the Word 2000 screen for the first time is sort of like trying to find your way through Tokyo's busy Ikebukuro subway station. It's intimidating. But once you start using Word, you quickly learn what everything is. In the meantime, the following table gives you some shorthand descriptions.

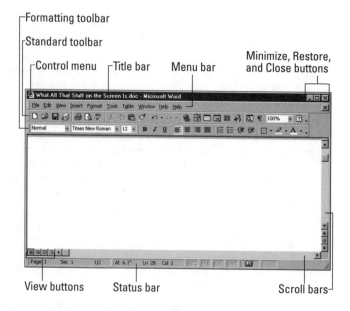

Part of Screen	What It Is
Title bar	At the top of the screen, the title bar tells you the name of the document you're working on.
Control menu	Click here to pull down a menu with options for minimizing, maximizing, moving, and closing the window.
Minimize, Restore, Close buttons	These three magic buttons make it very easy to shrink, enlarge, and close the window you are working in.
Menu bar	The list of menu options, from File to Help, that you choose from to give commands.
Standard toolbar	Offers buttons that you click to execute commands.
Formatting toolbar	Offers formatting buttons and pull-down lists for changing the appearance or layout of text.
Scroll bars	The scroll bars help you get from place to place in a document. ***See also*** "Moving Around in Documents" in Part II to find out how to use them.
View buttons	Click one of these to change your view of a document. ***See also*** "Viewing Documents in Different Ways" in Part II.
Status bar	The status bar gives you basic information about where you are and what you're doing in a document. It tells you what page and what section you're in, the total number of pages in the document, and where the insertion point is on the page.

Understanding How Paragraphs Work

Back in English class, your teacher taught you that a paragraph is a part of a longer composition that presents one idea or, in the case of dialogue, presents the words of one speaker. Your teacher was right, too, but for word processing purposes, a paragraph is a lot less than that. In word processing, a paragraph is simply what you put on-screen before you press the Enter key.

For instance, a heading is a paragraph. So is a graphic. If you press Enter on a blank line to go to the next line, the blank line is considered a paragraph. If you type **Dear John** at the top of a letter and press Enter, "Dear John" is a paragraph.

 It's important to know this because paragraphs have a lot to do with formatting. If you choose the Format⇔Paragraph command and monkey around with the paragraph formatting, all your changes affect everything in the paragraph that the cursor is in. To make format changes to a whole paragraph, all you have to do is place the cursor there. You don't have to select the paragraph. And if you want to make format changes to several paragraphs in a row, all you have to do is select those paragraphs first.

Starting Word 2000

To start Word 2000, all you have to do is this:

1. Click the Start button on the taskbar. You find the Start button in the lower-left corner of your screen.

2. Choose Programs on the menu that appears.

3. Choose Microsoft Word.

Editing and Other Essentials

In Part II, you find instructions for editing and doing the tasks that take up most of your word processing time. Among other things, Part II explains how to create, open, and close files. It tells you how to move around in documents, cut and copy text, and hyphenate and fix spelling errors.

My Word, there are a lot of good things in Part II!

In this part . . .

- ✔ Deleting, selecting, cutting, copying, and pasting text
- ✔ Finding and correcting spelling errors
- ✔ Opening and closing a document
- ✔ Exiting Word 2000
- ✔ Saving a document
- ✔ Working with headers, footers, and page numbers
- ✔ Working with more than one document at once
- ✔ Zooming in and out on a document

Breaking a Line

You can break a line in the middle, before it reaches the right margin, without starting a new paragraph. To do that, press Shift+Enter.

By pressing Shift+Enter, you can fix problems in the way Word breaks lines. When words are squeezed into narrow columns, it often pays to break lines to remove ugly white spaces.

This figure shows two identical paragraphs. To make the lines break better, I pressed Shift+Enter before the word *in* in the first line of the paragraph on the right. I did it again in the second-to-last line before the word *annual*. As you can see, the paragraph on the right fits in the column better and is easier to read.

"A computer in every home and a chicken in every pot is our goal," stated Rupert T. Verguenza, President and CEO of the New Technics Corporation International at the annual shareholder meeting this week.	"A computer in every home and a chicken in every pot is our goal," stated Rupert T. Verguenza, President and CEO of the New Technics Corporation International at the annual shareholder meeting this week.

Line breaks are marked with the ↵ symbol. To erase line breaks, click the Show/Hide button to see these symbols and backspace over them.

Breaking a Page

Word gives you another page so that you can keep going when you fill up one page. But what if you're impatient and want to start a new page right away? Whatever you do, *don't* press Enter over and over until you fill up the page. Instead, create a page break by doing either of the following:

+ Press Ctrl+Enter.

+ Choose Insert⇨Break, click Page Break, and click OK.

In Normal View, you know when you've inserted a page break because you see the words Page Break and two dotted lines instead of a single dotted line at the end of the page. In Print Layout view, you can't tell where you inserted a page break. To delete a page break, switch to Normal View, click the words Page Break, and press the Delete key. Change views by clicking the View buttons in the lower-left corner of the screen.

Changing the Look of the Screen

The Word window is cluttered, to say the least, but you can do something about that with options on the View menu:

✦ To remove a toolbar, choose <u>V</u>iew➪<u>T</u>oolbars. In the submenu, check marks appear beside the toolbars currently showing. Click a toolbar name to remove the check mark and remove the toolbar from the screen as well. You can also remove a toolbar by right-clicking it or the menu bar and then clicking the name of the toolbar you want to remove on the shortcut menu.

✦ Choose <u>V</u>iew➪<u>R</u>uler to get rid of or display the ruler.

✦ Choose <u>V</u>iew➪F<u>u</u>ll Screen if you want to get rid of everything except the text you're working on. When you choose Full Screen, everything gets stripped away — buttons, menus, scroll bars, and all. Only a single button called Close Full Screen remains. Click it or press Esc when you want the buttons, menus, and so on to come back. As the following figure shows, you can give commands from the menus on the menu bar in Full Screen View by moving the pointer to the top of the screen to make the menu bar appear. Of course, you can also press shortcut key combinations and right-click to see shortcut menus.

Click to get Word back

Changing lowercase to UPPERCASE, UPPERCASE to lowercase

What do you do if you look at your screen and discover to your dismay that you entered characters IN THE WRONG CASE? It happens. And sometimes Word does mysterious things to letters at the start of sentences and capital letters in the middle of words.

What can you do about that?

You can fix uppercase and lowercase problems in two ways.

 The fastest way is to select the text you entered incorrectly and press Shift+F3. Keep pressing Shift+F3 until the text looks right. Shift+F3 changes the characters to all lowercase, to Initial Capitals, to ALL UPPERCASE, and back to all lowercase again.

The other way is to select the text, choose Format⇨Change Case, and click an option in the Change Case dialog box:

+ **Sentence case:** Makes the text look like this.

+ **lowercase:** makes the text look like this.

+ **UPPERCASE:** MAKES THE TEXT LOOK LIKE THIS.

+ **Title Case:** Makes The Text Look Like This.

+ **tOGGLE cASE:** mAKES THE TEXT LOOK LIKE THIS, AND i WOULD CHOOSE THIS OPTION IF i ACCIDENTALLY TYPED LOTS OF TEXT WITH CAPS LOCK ON.

 Microsoft Weird is very presumptuous about how it thinks capital letters should be used. You've probably noticed that already. You can't type a lowercase letter after a period. You can't enter a newfangled company name like QUestData because Word refuses to let two capital letters in a row stand. You can't enter lowercase computer code at the start of a line without Word capitalizing the first letter. *See also* "Correcting Typos on the Fly" in Part V if you want to change how Word deals with capital letters.

Closing a Document

 Click the Close Window button or choose File⇨Close to close a document when you're done working on it. The Close Window button is located in the upper-right corner of the screen, right below its identical twin, the Close button.

If you try to close a document and you've made changes to it that you haven't saved yet, a dialog box similar to this one asks if you want to save your changes:

Click Yes, unless you're abandoning the document because you want to start all over. In that case, click No.

Copying, Moving, and Pasting Text

Word offers a number of different ways to copy and move text from one place to another. By one place to another, I mean from one part of a document to another part, from one document to another document, and from one program to another program. Yes, you can even move and copy data between Windows-based programs.

When you copy or cut text with the Copy or Cut commands, the text is placed in an electronic holding tank in your computer called the *Clipboard*. From there, you can paste it into a new location. Here's the conventional way to move or copy text:

1. Select the text to move or copy.

2. Do one of the following:

- **To move:** Choose <u>E</u>dit⇨Cu<u>t</u>, click the Cut button, or press Ctrl+X to remove the text from your document and place it on the Clipboard. You can also right-click and choose Cu<u>t</u> from the shortcut menu.

- **To copy:** Choose <u>E</u>dit⇨<u>C</u>opy, click the Copy button, or press Ctrl+C to place a copy of the text on the Clipboard. You can also right-click and choose <u>P</u>aste from the shortcut menu.

3. Place the cursor where you want to move or copy the text.

4. Choose <u>E</u>dit⇨<u>P</u>aste, click the Paste button, or press Ctrl+V to paste the text into your document. Or right-click and choose <u>P</u>aste.

The Clipboard can hold the last 12 items that you cut or copied. To paste in an item that you cut some time ago from a document, choose <u>V</u>iew⇨<u>T</u>oolbars⇨Clipboard (or right-click a toolbar and choose Clipboard). On the Clipboard toolbar, slowly move the pointer over the "scrap" icons until you see the first few words of the item you want to paste in your document, and then click.

The Clipboard toolbar also offers the Copy button for copying text, a button for pasting in all the scraps at once, and a button for emptying out the Clipboard.

Yet another, even speedier way to move or copy text is to use the drag-and-drop method:

1. Select the text you want to copy or move.

2. Slide the mouse over the selected text until the cursor changes into an arrow.

3. Copy or move the text:

- **To move:** Drag the text to a new location. As you drag, a small square appears below the mouse pointer to show that you are moving text.

- **To copy:** Hold down the Ctrl key while you drag the text elsewhere. A square with a cross in it appears below the pointer.

4. At the place where you want to move or copy the text, let up on the mouse button.

One neat thing about dragging and dropping is that you can copy or move text without disturbing what's on the Clipboard. Text isn't copied to the Clipboard when you drag and drop.

Creating a New Document

There are three ways to create a brand-new document:

♦ Choose File➪New.

♦ Press Ctrl+N.

♦ Click the New Blank Document button.

If you opt for File➪New, you see the New dialog box with tabs, icons, and wizards for creating documents from templates. A *template* is a ready-made layout that you can use for formatting a document. A *wizard* is a series of dialog boxes in which you make choices about the kind of document you want. If you are in the market for a fancy document, you can save a lot of time by doing it with a template or a wizard, because you don't have to do the formatting yourself.

In the New dialog box, click a tab, choose a template or wizard, and click OK. Be sure to look in the Preview box to see roughly what your document will look like when you are done creating it.

Watch this box!

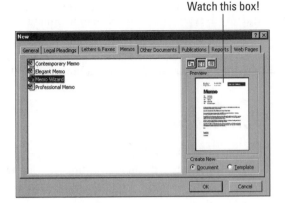

Dashes

You can spot the work of an amateur because amateurs always use a hyphen when they ought to use an em dash and en dash. An *em dash* looks like a hyphen but is wider — it's as wide as the letter *m*. The last sentence has an em dash in it. Did you notice?

An *en dash* is the width of the letter *n*. Use en dashes to show inclusive numbers or time periods, like so: pp. 45–50, Aug.–Sept. 1998, Exodus 16:11–16:18. An en dash is a little bit longer than a hyphen.

To place em or en dashes in your documents and impress your local typesetter or editor, not to mention your readers:

1. Choose Insert⇨Symbol.

2. Click the Special Characters tab in the Symbol dialog box.

3. Choose Em Dash or En Dash.

4. Click Insert and then click the Close button.

Another way to create an em dash is by typing two hyphens in a row. Word turns them into a single em dash. You can also press Alt+Ctrl+- (the minus sign key on the Numeric keypad) to enter an em dash, or Ctrl+- (on the numeric keypad) to enter an en dash.

Deleting Text

To delete a bunch of text at once, select the text you want to delete and press the Delete key or choose Edit⇨Clear.

By the way, you can kill two birds with one stone by selecting text and then starting to type. The letters you type immediately take the place of and delete the text you selected.

See also "Undoing a Mistake" later in this part if you delete text and realize to your horror and dismay that you shouldn't have done that.

Deleting a Word Document

Deleting documents is really the duty of the Windows operating system, but you can delete a document without leaving Word by following these steps:

1. Choose File⇨Open as if you were opening a document, not deleting one.

2. In the Open dialog box, find the document you want to delete.

3. Either click the Delete button at the top of the dialog box or press the Delete key. You can also right-click and choose Delete from the shortcut menu.

4. When Word asks if you really want to go through with it and send the file to the Recycle Bin, click Yes.

5. Click Cancel or press Esc to remove the Open dialog box.

Delete button

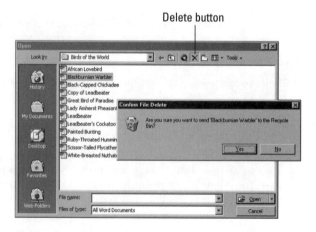

If you regret deleting a file, you can resuscitate it. On the Windows desktop, double-click the Recycle Bin icon. The Recycle Bin opens with a list of the files you deleted. Click the one you regret deleting and choose File⇨Restore.

Exiting Word 2000

When it's time to say good-bye to Word, save and close all your documents. Then do one of the following:

✦ Choose File➪Exit.

 ✦ Click the Close button (the X) on the right side of the title bar.

✦ Press Alt+F4.

If perchance you forgot to save and close a document, you see the dialog box that asks, Do you want to save the changes? Click Yes.

Finding and Replacing Text and Formats

The Edit➪Replace command is a very powerful tool indeed. If you're writing a Russian novel, and decide on page 816 to change the main character's last name from Oblonsky to Oblomov, you can change it on all 816 pages with the Edit➪Replace command in about a half a minute.

But here's the drawback: You never quite know what this command will do. Newspaper editors tell a story about a newspaper that made it a policy to use the word *African-American* instead of *black*. A laudable policy, except that a sleepy editor made the change with the Edit➪Replace command and didn't review it. Next day, a lead story on the business page read, "After years of running in the red, US Steel has paid all its debts, and now the corporation is running well in the African-American, according to company officials."

To replace words, phrases, or formats throughout a document:

1. Choose Edit➪Replace or press Ctrl+H.

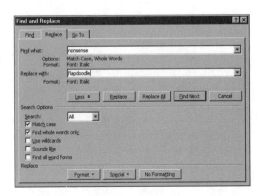

2. Fill in the Find What box just as you would if you were searching for text or formats, and be sure to click the Find Whole Words Only check box if you want to replace one word with another. (*See also* "Finding Text and More" later in this part to find out how to conduct a search.)

3. In the Replace With box, enter the text that will replace what is in the Find What box. If you're replacing a format, enter the format.

4. Either replace everything at once or do it one at a time:

- Click Replace All to make all replacements in an instant.

- Click Find Next and then either click Replace to make the replacement or Find Next to bypass it.

Word tells you when you're finished.

The sleepy newspaper editor I told you about clicked the Replace All button. Only do that if you're very confident and know exactly what you're doing. In fact, one way to keep from making embarrassing replacements is to start by using the Edit➪Find command. When you land on the first instance of the thing you're searching for, click the Replace tab and tell Word what should replace the thing you found. This way, you can rest assured that you entered the right search criteria and that Word is finding exactly what you want it to find.

The Edit➪Replace command is very powerful. *Always* save your document before you use this command. Then, if you replace text that you shouldn't have replaced, you can close your document without saving it, open your document again, and get your original document back.

Finding Text and More

You can search for a word in a document, and even for fonts, special characters, and formats. Here's how:

1. Choose Edit➪Find, press Ctrl+F, or click the Select Browse Object button in the lower-right corner of the screen and choose Find. The Find and Replace dialog box appears (in this figure, the More button is clicked so that you can see all the Find options).

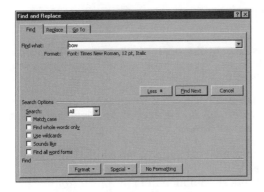

2. Enter the word, phrase, or format that you're looking for in the Find What dialog box (I explain how to enter formats later in this section). The words and phrases you looked for recently are on the Find What drop-down list. Click the down arrow to view and make a selection from that list if you want to.

3. Click the Find Next button if you are looking for a simple word or phrase. Otherwise, click the More button to conduct a sophisticated search before you click Find Next.

If the thing you're looking for can be found, Word highlights it in the document. To find the next instance of the thing you are looking for, click Find Next again. You can also close the dialog box and click either the Previous Find/Go To or Next Find/Go To button at the bottom of the scroll bar to the right of the screen (or press Ctrl+Page Up or Ctrl+Page Down) to go to the previous or next instance of the thing you are looking for.

By clicking the More button in the Find and Replace dialog box, you can get very selective about what to search for and how to search for it:

✦ **Search:** Click the down arrow and choose All, Up, or Down to search the whole document, search from the cursor position upward, or search from the cursor position downward, respectively.

✦ **Match Case:** Searches for words with uppercase and lowercase letters that exactly match those in the Find What box. With this box selected, a search for *bow* finds that word, but not *Bow* or *BOW*.

✦ **Find Whole Words Only:** Normally, a search for *bow* yields *elbow, bowler, bow-wow,* and all other words with the letters *b-o-w* (in that order). Click this option and you get only *bow*.

✦ **Use Wildcards:** Click here if you intend to use wildcards in searches.

✦ **Sounds Like:** Looks for words that sound like the one in the Find What box. A search for *bow* with this option selected finds *beau,* for example.

✦ **Find All Word Forms:** Takes into account verb endings and plurals. With this option clicked, you get *bows, bowing,* and *bowed,* as well as *bow.*

To search for words, paragraphs, tab settings, and styles, among other things, that are formatted a certain way, click the Format button and choose an option from the menu. You see the familiar dialog box you used in the first place to format the text. In the Find dialog box shown in this book, I chose Font from the Format menu and filled in the Font dialog box in order to search for the word "bow" in Times New Roman, 12-point, italicized font.

Click the Special button to look for format characters, manual page breaks, and other unusual stuff.

That No Formatting button is there so that you can clear all the formatting from the Find What box. Once you've found something, you can give Word instructions for replacing it by clicking the Replace tab. To find out about that, you have to read "Finding and Replacing Text and Formats," also in this part.

After you click the More button to get at the sophisticated search options, the button changes its name to Less. In this instance, More is Less. Click the Less button to shrink the dialog box and get more room to work on-screen.

Getting the Help You Need

Word offers a bunch of different ways to get help, and one or two of them are useful. The best way to get help is to choose Help⇨Contents and Index. That takes you to a dialog box with three tabs for finding the instructions you need:

✦ **Contents:** A bunch of general topics. Double-click a book icon, and it opens to more topics, each with a question mark beside its name. Click the question mark beside the topic that interests you and click Display, if general topics are your cup of tea.

✦ **Index:** This is the most useful means of getting help. Click the Index tab and type a few letters that describe what puzzles you. The alphabetical list of index topics scrolls down to show you which topics are available. If a topic strikes your fancy, double-click it or click it and choose Display. You'll go straight to an informative instruction box or some other help feature.

✦ **Find:** With this option, you search for a word in the Help files. For example, if you need help with entering accented characters, type **accent**. A list of topics appears at the bottom of the dialog box. Click the topic you're interested in and click Display.

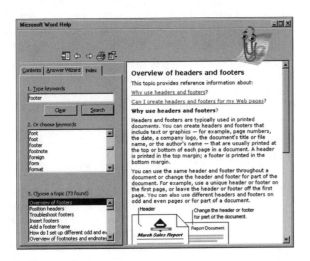

Another useful way to get help is to choose Help⇨What's This or press Shift+F1.The pointer changes into an arrow with a question mark beside it. Click this quizzical cursor on a part of the screen that you want to know more about. With any luck, you get concise instructions for carrying out the thing you clicked. Here is the mini-Help screen you get when you click text to see how it is formatted:

HELP ME PLEASE

The upper-right corner of dialog boxes also have Help buttons in the shape of question marks. Click a dialog box Help button and click the part of the dialog box you need help with to get a brief explanation of the thing you clicked.

In keeping with its goal of making computers as much fun to use as watching Saturday morning cartoons, Microsoft also offers the Office Assistant. Click the Microsoft Word Help button on the Standard toolbar (or press F1), and the Office Assistant — a dog named Rover — appears in a corner of the screen, along with a bubble caption into which you can type a question. Type your question, click Search, and hope for a sensible answer. Choose Help⇨Hide the Office Assistant when you want Rover to go away.

Yet another way to seek help is to find it on the Internet. Choose Help⇨Office on the Web to go to the official Microsoft Office Web site, where you can get advice about using Word and even submit questions to Microsoft technicians (but don't expect an answer right away).

Hyphenating a Document

The first thing you should know about hyphenating the words in a document is that you may not need to do it. Text that hasn't been hyphenated is sometimes easier to read. The text in this book has what typesetters call a *ragged right margin,* which makes for very few hyphenated words. Hyphenate only when text is trapped in columns or in other narrow places or when you want a very formal-looking document.

 You can hyphenate text as you enter it, but I think you should wait until you've written everything so that you can concentrate on the words themselves. Then when you're done with the writing, you can either have Word hyphenate the document automatically or you can do it yourself.

Hyphenating a document automatically

To hyphenate a document automatically:

1. Choose Tools⇨Language⇨Hyphenation.

2. Click Automatically Hyphenate Document to let Word do the job.

3. Click Hyphenate Words in CAPS to remove the check mark if you don't care to hyphenate words in uppercase.

4. If the text isn't justified — that is, if it's "ragged right" — you can play with the Hyphenation Zone setting (but I don't think you should hyphenate ragged right text anyway). Words that fall in the Zone are hyphenated, so a large zone means a less ragged margin but more ugly hyphens, and a small zone means fewer ugly hyphens but a more ragged right margin.

5. More than two consecutive hyphens in a row on the right margin looks bad, so enter **2** in the Limit Consecutive Hyphens To box.

6. Click OK.

Hyphenating a document manually

The other way to hyphenate is to see where Word wants to put hyphens and "Yea" or "Nay" them one at a time:

1. Select the part of the document you want to hyphenate, or else place the cursor where you want hyphens to start appearing.

2. Choose Tools⇨Language⇨Hyphenation.

3. Click the Manual button. Word displays a box with some hyphenation choices in it. The cursor blinks on the spot where Word suggests putting a hyphen.

4. Click Yes or No to accept or reject Word's suggestion.

5. Keep accepting or rejecting Word's suggestions. A box appears to tell you when Word has finished hyphenating. To quit hyphenating yourself, click the Cancel button in the Manual Hyphenation dialog box.

A fast way to insert a manual hyphen is to put the cursor where you want the hyphen to go and press Ctrl+hyphen. Press Ctrl+hyphen when there is a big gap in the right margin and a word is crying out to be hyphenated. In this illustration, I pressed Ctrl+hyphen after "antidisestablishmen" in the paragraph on the left to make the line break in a better position, as shown in the paragraph on the right.

| On a "ragged right" margin, how do you fix the gaps that appear when you use long words like "antidisestablishmentarianism?" You press Ctrl+hyphen, that's how. | On a "ragged right" margin, how do you fix the gaps that appear when you use long words like "antidisestablishmen-tarianism?" You press Ctrl+hyphen, that's how. |

By pressing Ctrl+hyphen, you tell Word to make the hyphen appear only if the word breaks at the end of a line. Do not insert a hyphen simply by pressing the hyphen key, because the hyphen will stay there even if the word appears in the middle of a line and doesn't need to be broken in half.

Unhyphenating and other hyphenation tasks

More hyphenation esoterica:

✦ To "unhyphenate" a document you hyphenated automatically, choose Tools⇨Language⇨Hyphenation, remove the check from the Automatically Hyphenate Document box, and click OK. To remove manual hyphens, delete or backspace over them.

✦ To prevent a paragraph from being hyphenated, choose Format⇨Paragraph, click the Line and Page Breaks tab, and put a check mark in the Don't Hyphenate box. If you can't hyphenate a paragraph, it's probably because this box was checked unintentionally.

✦ To hyphenate a single paragraph in the middle of a document — maybe because it's a long quotation or some other thing that needs to stand out — select the paragraph and hyphenate it manually by clicking the Manual button in the Hyphenation dialog box.

Inserting a Whole File in a Document

One of the beautiful things about word processing is that you can recycle documents. Say you wrote an essay on the Scissor-Tailed Flycatcher that would fit very nicely in a broader report on North American birds. You can insert the Scissor-Tailed Flycatcher document into your report document:

1. Place the cursor where you want to insert the document.

2. Choose Insert⇨File.

3. In the Insert File dialog box, find and click the file you want to insert.

4. Click the Insert button.

Moving Around in Documents

Documents have a habit of getting longer and longer, and as they do that it takes more effort to move around in them. Here are some shortcuts for getting here and there in documents.

Keys for getting around quickly

One of the fastest ways to go from place to place is to press keys and key combinations:

Key to Press	Where It Takes You
PgUp	Up the length of one screen
PgDn	Down the length of one screen
Ctrl+PgUp	To the previous page in the document
Ctrl+PgDn	To the next page in the document
Ctrl+Home	To the top of the document
Ctrl+End	To the bottom of the document

If pressing Ctrl+PgUp or Ctrl+PgDn doesn't get you to the top or bottom of a page, it's because you clicked the Select Browse Object button at the bottom of the vertical scroll bar, so Word goes to the next bookmark, comment, heading, or whatever. Click the Select Browse Object button and choose Browse by Page to make these key combinations work again.

Zipping around with the scroll bar

You can also use the scroll bar to get around in documents. The *scroll bar* is the vertical stripe along the right side of the screen that resembles an elevator shaft. Here's how to move around with the scroll bar:

- ✦ To move through a document quickly, grab the elevator (called the *scroll box*) and drag it up or down. As you scroll, a box appears with the page number and the names of headings on the pages you scroll past (provided that you assigned Word styles to those headings).

- ✦ To move line by line up or down, click the up or down arrow at the top or bottom of the scroll bar.

- ✦ To move screen by screen, click anywhere on the scroll bar except on the arrows or the elevator.

By the way, the scroll bar on the bottom of the screen is for moving from side to side.

See also "Going Here, Going There in Documents" and "Bookmarks for Hopping Around" in Part V for more moving around shortcuts.

Numbering the Pages

Word numbers the pages of a document automatically, which is great, but if your document has a title page and table of contents and you want to start numbering pages on the fifth page, or if your document has more than one section, page numbers can turn into a sticky business.

The first thing to ask yourself is whether you've included headers or footers in your document. If you have, go to "Putting Headers and Footers on Pages," later in this part. It explains how to put page numbers in a header or footer.

Meantime, use the Insert⇨Page Numbers command to put plain old page numbers on the pages of a document:

1. Choose Insert⇨Page Numbers to open the Page Numbers dialog box.

Where the page number goes

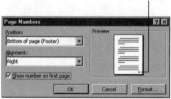

2. In the Position and Alignment boxes, choose where you want the page number to appear. The lovely Preview box on the right shows where your page number will go.

3. Click to remove the check mark from the <u>S</u>how Number on First Page box if you're working on a letter or other type of document that usually doesn't have a number on page 1.

4. Click OK.

If you want to get fancy, I should warn you that it's easier to do that in headers and footers than it is in the Page Numbers dialog box. Follow the first three steps in the preceding list and click the Format button. Then, in the Page Number Format dialog box, choose an option:

✦ **Number Format:** Choose a new way to number the pages if you want to. (Notice the *i,ii,iii* choice. That's how the start of books, this one included, are numbered.)

✦ **Include Chapter Number:** Click this check box if you want to start numbering pages anew at the beginning of each chapter. Pages in Chapter 1, for example, are numbered 1-1, 1-2, and so on, and pages in Chapter 2 are numbered 2-1, 2-2, and so forth.

✦ **Chapter Starts with Style:** If necessary, choose a heading style from the drop-down list to tell Word where new chapters begin. Chapter titles are usually tagged with the Heading 1 style, but if your chapters begin with another style, choose that style from the list.

✦ **Use Separator:** From the list, tell Word how you want to separate the chapter number from the page number. Choose the hyphen (1-1), period (1.1), colon (1:1), or one of the dashes (1—1).

✦ **Page Numbering:** This is the one that matters if you've divided your document into sections. Either start numbering the pages anew and enter a new page number to start at (probably 1), or else number pages where the previous section left off.

When you finish, click OK twice to number the pages and get back to your document.

To get rid of the page numbers if you don't like them, follow these steps:

1. Either choose <u>V</u>iew⇨<u>H</u>eader and Footer or double-click the page number in Print Layout view.

2. Click the Switch Between Header and Footer button, if necessary, to get to the footer.

3. Select the page number by clicking it, and then press the Delete key. You may have to click the number a couple of times to select it properly. You know the number is selected when black squares appear around it.

Opening a Document

Before you can start working on a document that you have created and named, you have to open it. And because finding the file you want to open can sometimes be difficult, Word offers several amenities to help you locate files and quickly open them.

The conventional way to open a document

Following is the conventional method of opening a document:

1. Choose <u>F</u>ile⇨<u>O</u>pen, press Ctrl+O, or click the Open button.

2. Find the folder that holds the file you want to open. To do that, try using these nifty tools:

- **Look <u>I</u>n drop-down menu:** Click the down arrow to open the Look <u>I</u>n drop-down menu, and then click a drive letter or folder to see its contents.

- **Back button:** If you stray too far in your search, click the Back button to see the folder you looked at previously.

- **Up One Level button:** Click the Up One Level button to climb up the hierarchy of folders on your computer system.

- **Views button and menu:** Click the Views down arrow and choose an option to examine the contents of a folder more closely. The List option on the menu lists filenames, the Details option tells how large files are and when they were last modified, the Properties option provides details about the file selected in the dialog box, and the Preview option shows the file. You can also click the Views button to cycle through the choices on the menu.

- **Folders:** Double-click a folder to place its name in the Look <u>I</u>n box and see its contents.

3. When you've found the folder and it is listed in the Look In box, click the name of the file you want to open.

4. Either double-click the file you selected or click the Open button.

Double-click to see folder's contents

Back button

Click to choose a new drive or folder

Up One Level button

View button

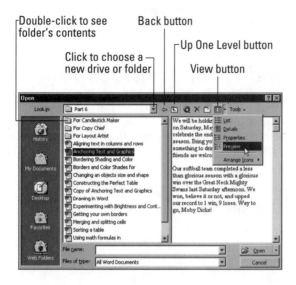

Speed techniques for opening documents

Rooting around in the Open dialog box to find a document is a bother, so Word offers these handy buttons that you can click to find and open documents:

Click This Button	To See
History	The last three dozen documents and folders that you opened. Double-click a document to reopen it; double-click a folder to see its contents.
My Documents	The contents of the My Documents folder. Double-click a document to open it. The My Documents folder is a good place to keep documents you are currently working on. When you're done with a current document, you can move it to a different folder for safekeeping.
Favorites	The Favorites folder with its shortcuts to files and folders that you go to often. Double-click a shortcut icon to open a document or folder. To create a shortcut to a document and place it in the Favorites folder, find and click the document in the Open dialog box, click the Tools down arrow, and choose Add to Favorites. (To remove a shortcut icon, click it and then click the Delete button. By doing so, you delete the shortcut, not the document or folder itself.)

If you want to open a document you worked on recently, it may be on the File menu. Check it out. Open the File menu and see whether the document you want to open is one of the four listed at the bottom of the menu. If it is, click its name or press its number (1 through 4). To list more than four files at the bottom of the menu, choose Tools⇨Options, click the General tab in the Options dialog box, and enter a number higher than 4 in the Recently Used File List scroll box.

Putting Headers and Footers on Pages

A *header* is a little description that appears along the top of a page so that the reader knows what's what. Usually, headers include the page number and a title. A *footer* is the same thing as a header, except that it appears along the bottom of the page, as befits its name.

To put a header or a footer in a document, follow these steps:

1. Choose View⇨Header and Footer.

2. Type your header in the box or, if you want a footer, click the Switch between Header and Footer button and type your footer.

3. Click the Close button.

While you're typing away in the Header or Footer box, you can call on most of the commands on the Standard and Formatting toolbars. You can change the text's font and font size, click an alignment button, and paste text from the Clipboard.

You can also take advantage of these buttons on the Header and Footer toolbar:

Button	What It Does
Insert AutoText ▾	Opens a drop-down menu with options for inserting information about the document, including when it was last saved and printed, and who created it.
⊞	Inserts the page number.

Button	What It Does
	Inserts the number of pages in the entire document. On the right side of the sample header shown in the previous figure, I pressed the Insert Page Number button and typed the word *of* and a space, then pressed the Insert Number of Pages button so that readers know the length of the document as well as what page they are on.
	Opens the Page Number Format dialog box so you can choose a format for the page number in the header or footer. ***See also*** "Numbering the Pages" earlier in this part to find out how this dialog box works.
	These buttons insert the date the document is printed and the time it is printed into the header or footer.
	Opens the Layout tab of the Page Setup dialog box so that you can tell Word that you want a different header and footer on the first page of the document, or that you want different headers and footers on odd and even pages (you might use this feature if you're printing on both sides of the page).
	Shows the text on the page so that you can see what the header or footer looks like in relation to the text.
	Tells Word that you don't want this header or footer to be the same as the header or footer in the previous section of the document. When this button is pressed down, the header or footer is the same as the header or footer in the previous section of the document, and the Header or Footer box reads, "Same as Previous." To enter a different header or footer for a section, click this button and enter the header or footer. To change headers or footers, you must divide a document into sections (***see also*** "Dividing a Document into Sections" in Part III).
	Switches between the header and the footer.
	Shows the header or footer in the previous and next sections of a document that has more than one section.

Removing headers and footers is as easy as falling off a turnip truck:

1. Click View⇨Header and Footer or double-click the header or footer in Print Layout View.

2. Select the header or footer.

3. Press the Delete key.

To remove the header and footer from the first page of either a document or a section, choose File➪Page Setup (or click the Page Setup button on the Header and Footer toolbar). In the Page Setup dialog box, click the Layout tab, click the Different First Page check box, and click OK.

Renaming a Document

If the name you gave to a document suddenly seems inappropriate or downright meaningless, you can rename it. Here's how:

1. Choose File➪Open, press Ctrl+O, or click the Open button.

2. In the Open dialog box, find the folder that holds the file you want to rename. (*See also* "Opening a Document" earlier in this part if you need help finding the folder.)

3. Click the file you want to rename.

4. Click the Tools button and choose Rename from the drop-down list.

5. The old name is highlighted. Enter a new name in its place.

6. Press the Enter key.

Saving a Document for the First Time

After you open a new document and work on it, you need to save it. As part of saving a document for the first time, Word opens a dialog box and invites you to give the document a name. So the first time you save, you do three things at once — you save your work, choose which folder to save the document in, and name your document.

To save a document for the first time:

1. Choose File➪Save, press Ctrl+S, or click the Save button.

2. Find and select the folder that you want to save the file in. (*See also* "Opening a Document" earlier in this part if you need help finding folders. The same techniques for finding folders apply in the Open and Save As dialog boxes.)

3. Word suggests a name in the File Name box (the name comes from the first line in the document). If that name isn't suitable, enter another. Be sure to enter one you will remember later.

4. Click the Save button.

Document names can be 255 characters long and can include all characters and numbers except these: / ? : * " < > |. They can even include spaces.

Saving a Document under a New Name

If you want to make a second copy of a document, you can do so by saving the first copy under a new name or by making a copy. Either way you end up with two copies of the same file. To save a document under a new name:

1. Choose File⇨Save As.

2. Find and select a folder to save the newly named document in. (*See also* "Opening a Document" earlier in this part if you need help locating folders.)

3. Give the document a new name in the File Name text box.

4. If you're also changing the type of file this is, click the Save as Type drop-down list and choose the file type. *See also* "Importing and Exporting Files" in Part VIII if you need to know more about file types.

5. Click the Save button.

To save a copy of a document, open it as you normally would, but click the down arrow next to the Open button in the Open dialog box and select Open as Copy from the drop-down list. The new document is given the same name as the old, except the words "Copy of" appear in front of its name.

Saving a Document You've Been Working On

It behooves you to save your documents from time to time as you work on them. (No, *behooves* is not computer jargon. The word just means that you should.) When you save a document, Word takes the work you've done since the last time you saved your document and stores the work safely on the hard disk.

You can save a document in three different ways:

✦ Choose File➪Save.

 ✦ Click the Save button.

✦ Press Ctrl+S.

Save early and often. Make it a habit to click the Save button whenever you leave your desk, take a phone call, or let the cat out. If you don't save your work and there is a power outage or somebody trips over the computer's power cord, you lose all the work you did since the last time you saved your document.

Saving Versions of Documents

In a lengthy document like a manual or a report that requires many drafts, saving different drafts can be helpful. That way, if you want to retrieve something that got dropped from an earlier draft, you can do so. One way to save drafts of a document is to save drafts under different names, but why do that when you can rely on the Versions command on the File menu?

Follow these steps to save different versions of a document as it evolves into a masterpiece:

1. Choose File➪Versions. The Versions In dialog box, which lists past versions of the document that you saved, appears.

2. Click the Save Now button.

3. In the Save Version dialog box, write a descriptive comment about this version of the document and click OK.

4. Click Close in the Versions In dialog box.

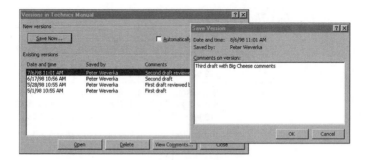

To review an earlier version of a document, choose File⇨Versions to open the Versions In dialog box, read comments to find the version you want to open, select the versions, and click the Open button. The earlier version appears in its own window next to the up-to-date version. You can tell which version you are dealing with by glancing at the title bar, which lists the date that the earlier version was saved.

Select a version and click the Delete button in the Versions In dialog box to erase a version; click the View Comments button to read its description. The Versions In dialog box also offers a check box for saving a version of the document each time you close it, but I don't recommend saving versions automatically. When you do so, you don't get the opportunity to describe the document, which makes it very hard to tell which draft is which when you want to revisit a draft you worked on before.

Selecting Text in Speedy Ways

To move text or copy it from one place to another, you have to select it first. You can also erase a great gob of text merely by selecting it and pressing the Delete key. So it pays to know how to select text. Here are some shortcuts for doing it:

To Select This	Do This
A word	Double-click the word.
A line	Click in the left margin next to the line.
Some lines	Drag the mouse over the lines or drag the mouse pointer down the left margin.
A paragraph	Double-click in the left margin next to the paragraph.
A mess of text	Click at the start of the text, hold down the Shift key, and click at the end of the text.

(continued)

To Select This	Do This
A gob of text	Put the cursor where you want to start selecting, press F8 or double-click EXT (it stands for Extend) on the status bar, and press an arrow key, drag the mouse, or click at the end of the selection.
Yet more text	If you select text and realize that you want to select yet more text, double-click EXT on the status bar and start dragging the mouse or pressing arrow keys.
A document	Hold down the Ctrl key and click in the left margin, or triple-click in the left margin, or choose Edit⇨Select All, or press Ctrl+A.

If you have a bunch of highlighted text on-screen and you want it to go away but it won't (because you pressed F8 or double-clicked EXT to select it), double-click EXT again.

After you press F8 or double-click EXT, all the keyboard shortcuts for moving the cursor also work for selecting text. For example, press F8 and press Ctrl+Home to select everything from the cursor to the top of the document. Double-click EXT and press End to select to the end of the line.

Spacing Lines

To change the spacing between lines, select the lines whose spacing you want to change or simply put the cursor in a paragraph if you're changing the line spacing in a single paragraph. (If you're just starting a document, you're ready to go.)

Choose Format⇨Paragraph and select an option in the Line Spacing drop-down list:

✦ **Single, 1.5 Lines, Double:** These three options are quite up front about what they do, and self-explanatory, too.

✦ **At Least:** Choose this one if you want Word to adjust for tall symbols or other unusual text. Word adjusts the lines but makes sure there is, at minimum, the number of points you enter in the At box between each line.

✦ **Exactly:** Choose this one and enter a number in the At box if you want a specific amount of space between lines.

✦ **Multiple:** Choose this one and put a number in the At box to get triple-, quadruple-, quintuple-, or any other spaced lines.

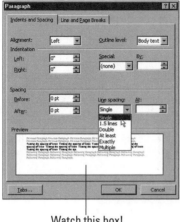

Watch this box!

You can get a sneak preview of what your lines look like by glancing at the Preview box. Click OK when you've made your choice.

To quickly single-space text, select it and press Ctrl+1. To quickly double-space text, select the text and press Ctrl+2.

You may notice the Before and After boxes in the Spacing area on the Indents and Spacing tab of the Paragraph dialog box. Use these boxes if you want to automatically insert blank space between paragraphs. But I must warn you that, to Word's mind, a heading is also a paragraph, so if you put space between paragraphs you may get strange blank spaces around your headings. And if you put space before *and* after paragraphs, you get twice the amount of space between paragraphs that you bargained for. The Before and After boxes are for use with styles, when a certain style of paragraph is always preceded by or followed by a specific amount of space.

Spell-Checking (And Grammar-Checking) a Document

As you must have noticed by now, red wiggly lines appear under words that are misspelled, and green wiggly lines appear under words and sentences that Word thinks are grammatically incorrect. Correct spelling and grammar errors by right-clicking them and choosing an option from the shortcut menu. If the red or green lines annoy you, you can remove them from the screen. Choose Tools⇨Options, click the Spelling & Grammar tab, and click to remove the check marks from Check Spelling as You Type or Check Grammar as You Type options.

That's the one-at-a-time method for correcting misspelled words and grammatical errors. You can also go the whole hog and spell- or grammar-check an entire document or text selection by starting in one of these ways:

✦ Choose Tools➪Spelling and Grammar.

✦ Press F7.

 ✦ Click the Spelling and Grammar button.

The Spelling and Grammar dialog box appears. Spelling errors appear in red type in this dialog box. Grammatical errors are colored green.

Correcting misspellings

Here are your options for handling red spelling errors:

✦ **Not in Dictionary:** Shows the word that is spelled incorrectly in context. You can click the scroll arrows in this box to see preceding or following text.

✦ **Suggestions:** Provides a list of words to use in place of the misspelling. Click the word that you want to replace the misspelled one.

✦ **Ignore:** Ignores the misspelling, but stops on it again if it appears later in the document.

✦ **Ignore All:** Ignores the misspelling wherever it appears in the document. Not only that, it ignores it in all your other open documents.

✦ **Add:** Adds the word in the Not in Dictionary box to the words in the dictionary that Microsoft Word deems correct. Click this button the first time that the spell-checker stops on your last name to add your last name to the spelling dictionary.

✦ **Change:** Click this button to insert the word in the Suggestions box in your document in place of the misspelled word.

✦ **Delete:** The Delete button appears where the Change button is when the spell-checker finds two words in a row ("the the," for example). Click the Delete button to remove the second word.

✦ **Change All:** Changes not only this misspelling to the word in the Suggestions box, but all identical misspellings in the document.

✦ **AutoCorrect:** Adds the suggested spelling correction to the list of words that are corrected automatically as you type them (*see also* "Correcting Typos on the Fly" in Part V).

✦ **Undo:** Goes back to the last misspelling you corrected and gives you a chance to repent and try again.

You can click outside the Spelling dialog box and fool around in your document, in which case the Ignore button changes names and becomes Resume. Click the Resume button to start the spell-check again.

Suppose that you have a bunch of computer code or French language text that you would like the spell-checker to either ignore or check against its French dictionary instead of its English one. To tell the spell-checker how to handle text like that, select the text, choose Tools⇨Language⇨Set Language. In the Language dialog box, choose a new language for your words to be spell-checked against, or else click the Do Not Check Spelling or Grammar check box.

You probably shouldn't trust your smell-checker, because it can't catch all misspelled words. If you mean to type **middle** but type **fiddle** instead, the spell-checker won't catch the error because *fiddle* is a legitimate word. The moral is: If you're working on an important document, proofread it carefully. Don't rely on the spell-checker to catch all your smelling errors.

Fixing grammar errors

Word's Grammar Checker is theoretically able to correct grammatical mistakes in a document. Personally, I think the thing is of little use and don't recommend using it. And I'm not just saying that because I'm an editor and writer and I (supposedly) have mastered grammar. I just think that a machine can't tell what's good writing and what isn't. Period.

Anyhow, grammar errors appear in green in the top of the Spelling and Grammar dialog box, as shown in this figure.

Click the following buttons to fix errors with the robo-grammarian:

✦ **Suggestions:** Lists ways to correct the error. Click the correction you want to make.

✦ **Ignore:** Lets the error stand in your document.

✦ **Ignore Rule:** Ignores this grammatical error and all other grammatical errors of this type in this document and all open documents.

✦ **Next Sentence:** Ignores the error and takes you to the next sentence in the text.

✦ **Change:** Replaces the error with what is in the Suggestions box.

✦ **Undo:** Reverses your most recent correction.

 If you have confidence in your grammatical abilities, click the Check Grammar check box to remove the check mark and keep so-called grammatical errors from being flagged.

Symbols and Special Characters

 You can decorate your documents with all kinds of symbols and special characters — a death's head, a smiley face, the Yen symbol. To insert a symbol, click where you want it to go and do the following:

1. Choose Insert➪Symbol. The Symbol dialog box opens.

2. Click the Font drop-down list to choose a symbol set.

3. When you choose some fonts, a Subset drop-down menu appears. Choose a subset name from the list — Latin-1, for example — to help locate the symbol you are looking for.

4. Click a symbol. When you do so, you see a bigger picture of it on-screen.

5. Click Insert.

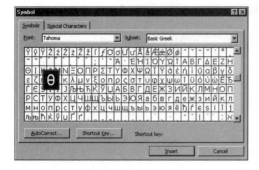

The symbol you choose is placed in your document, but the Symbol dialog box stays open so that you can select another symbol. Select another one, or click Close or press Esc when you are done.

You can choose special characters and unusual punctuation from the Special Characters tab of the Symbol dialog box.

Also in the Insert dialog box is the AutoCorrect button, which you can click to open the AutoCorrect dialog box and add the symbol you clicked to the list of symbols that Word inserts automatically (**see also** "Correcting Typos on the Fly" in Part V for the details). You can also click the Shortcut Key button to assign a keyboard shortcut to the symbol you clicked (**see also** "Customizing Word 2000," also in Part V).

The Thesaurus's Role in Finding the Right Word

If you can't seem to find the right word — if the word is on the tip of your tongue but you can't quite remember it — you can always give the Thesaurus a shot. To find synonyms (words that have the same or a similar meaning) for a word in your document, start by right-clicking the word and choosing Synonyms from the shortcut menu. With luck, the synonym you are looking for appears on the submenu and all you have to do is click to enter the synonym in your document. Usually, however, finding a good synonym is a journey, not a Sunday stroll. Follow these steps to search for a synonym:

1. Place the cursor in the word.

2. Choose Tools⇨Language⇨Thesaurus, or press Shift+F7.

3. Begin your quest for the right word.

4. When you find it, click it in the list of words in the Replace with Synonym box and then click the Replace button.

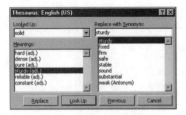

Finding the right words is nine-tenths of writing, so the Thesaurus dialog box tries to make it easier by offering these amenities:

✦ **Looked Up:** Provides a drop-down list with all the words you've investigated in your quest. To go back to a word you considered earlier, click it in this list or click the Previous button.

✦ **Meanings:** Lists different ways the term can be used — as a verb or noun, for example. Click here to turn your search in a different direction.

✦ **Replace with Synonym:** If the Thesaurus isn't being helpful, type a word into this box and click the Look Up button.

✦ **Look Up:** Click the Look Up button to investigate the word highlighted in the Replace with Synonym box scroll list.

At worst, if you know the opposite of the word you want, you can look it up in the Thesaurus and perhaps see its antonym listed in the Replace with Synonym box. That's one way to find the word you are looking for.

Undoing a Mistake

Fortunately for you, all is not lost if you make a big blunder in Word, because the program has a marvelous little tool called the Undo command.

This command "remembers" your last 99 editorial changes and puts them on the Undo drop-down list. As long as you catch your error before you do five or six new things, you can "undo" your mistake. Try one of these undo techniques:

✦ Choose Edit➪Undo. This command changes names, depending on what you did last. Usually, it says Undo Typing, but if you move text, for example, it says Undo Move. Anyhow, select this command to undo your most recent action.

✦ Click the Undo button to undo your most recent change. If you made your error and went on to do something else before you caught it, click the down arrow next to the Undo button. You see a menu of your last five actions. Click the one you want to undo or, if it isn't on the list, click the down-arrow on the scroll bar until you find the error, and then click on it. However, if you do this, you also undo all the actions on the Undo menu above the one you're undoing. For example, if you undo the 98th action on the list, you also undo the 97 before it.

What if you commit a monstrous error but can't correct it with the Undo command? You can try closing your document without saving the changes you made to it. As long as you didn't save your document after you made the error, the error won't be in your document when you open it again — but neither will the changes you want to keep.

Viewing Documents in Different Ways

In word processing, you want to focus sometimes on the writing, sometimes on the layout, and sometimes on the organization of your work. To help you stay in focus, Word offers different ways of viewing a document:

✦ **Normal view:** Choose View➪Normal or click the Normal View button (in the lower-left corner of the screen) when you want to focus on the words. Normal view is best for writing first drafts and proofreading.

✦ **Web Layout view:** Choose View➪Web Layout or click the Web Layout View button when you are creating a Web page. *See also* Part VI for an explanation of how to create Web pages with Word.

✦ **Print Layout view:** Choose View➪Print Layout or click the Print Layout View button to see the big picture. You can see graphics, headers, and footers, and even page borders in Print Layout view. Rulers appear on the window so that you can pinpoint where everything is.

> ✦ **Outline view:** Choose <u>V</u>iew⇨<u>O</u>utline or click the Outline View
> button to see how your work is organized. In Outline view, you
> see only the headings and the first lines of paragraphs. To see
> a document in Outline view, you must have assigned heading
> styles to headings in the document. *See also* "Outlines for
> Organizing Your Work" in Part V.

To keep text from straying off the right side of the screen in
Normal view and Outline view, you can tell Word to "wrap it" so
that you see all the text, no matter how long the lines in the
document are. To wrap text, choose <u>T</u>ools⇨<u>O</u>ptions, click the View
tab, and click the Wrap to Window check box in the Outline and
Normal Options part of the tab. If you choose this option, just
remember that the document on-screen is not the same as the one
you will print, because lines break in different places on-screen
than they do on paper.

Working on Many Documents at Once

In Word, you can work on more than one document at the same
time. You can even work in two different places in the same
document (the next entry in this book tells how).

When you open a new document, a new button is placed on the
taskbar. To go from one document to another, click its taskbar
button. You can also open the Window menu and click the name of
a document to see it on-screen. And if you want to see all open
documents at once, choose <u>W</u>indow⇨<u>A</u>rrange All. To go from one
document to the next, either click in a new window pane or press
Ctrl+F6.

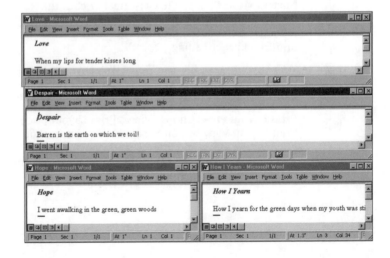

To focus on one window when several are open, click the Minimize button of the window panes you don't want to see anymore. By doing so, you remove the other documents from the screen. Click the Restore button (the one in the middle with a square on it) to enlarge the window you want to work on to full-screen size.

To see a window you minimized, either open the Window menu again and choose it from the menu or click a taskbar button.

Working in Two Places in the Same Document

You can open a window on two different places at once in a document. One reason you might do this: You are writing a long report and want the introduction to support the conclusion, and you also want the conclusion to fulfill all promises made by the introduction. That's difficult to do sometimes, but you can make it easier by opening the document to both places and writing the conclusion and introduction at the same time.

You can use two methods to open the same document to two different places: opening a second window on the document or splitting the screen.

Opening a second window

To open a second window on a document, choose Window⇨ New Window. Immediately, a second window opens up and you see the start of your document.

✦ If you select the Window menu, you see that it now lists two versions of your document, number 1 and number 2 (the numbers appear after the filename). Choose number 1 to go back to where you were before. You can also click a taskbar button to go from window to window.

✦ You can move around in either window as you please. When you make changes in either window, you make them to the same document. Choose the File⇨Save command in either window, and you save all the changes you made in both windows. The important thing to remember here is that you are working on a single document, not two documents.

 ✦ When you want to close either window, just click its Close button. You go back to the other window, and only one version of your document appears on the Window menu.

Splitting the screen

Splitting a window means to divide it into north and south halves. To do that, choose Window⇨Split. A gray line appears on-screen. Roll the mouse down until the gray line is where you want the split to be, and click. You get two screens split down the middle:

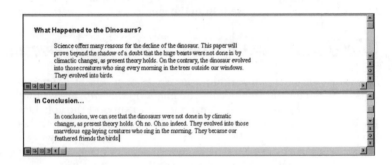

Now you have two windows and two sets of scroll bars along the right side of the screen.

✦ Use the scroll bars to move up or down on either side of the split, or press PgUp or PgDn, or press arrow keys. Click the other side if you want to move the cursor there.

✦ When you tire of this schizophrenic arrangement, choose Window⇨Remove Split or drag the gray line to the top or bottom of the screen.

You can also split a screen by moving the mouse cursor to the top of the scroll bar on the right. Move it just above the arrow. When it turns into a funny shape, something like a German cross, click and drag the gray line down the screen. When you release the mouse button, you have a split screen. To quickly "unsplit" a screen, double-click the line that splits the screen in two.

Zooming In, Zooming Out

Eyes were not meant to stare at computer screens all day, which makes the Zoom command all the more valuable. Use this command freely and often to enlarge or shrink the text on your screen and preserve your eyes for important things, like gazing at the horizon.

Give this command in one of two ways:

+ Click the down arrow in the Zoom box on the Standard toolbar (the box on the right side that shows a number followed by a percent sign) and choose a magnification percentage from the drop-down list.

+ Click inside the Zoom box, type a percentage of your own, and press Enter.

Enter or check a zoom percentage here

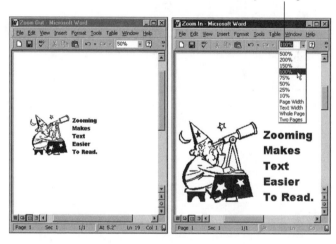

Sometimes it pays to shrink the text way down to see how pages are laid out. For instance, after you lay out a table, shrink it down to see how it looks from a bird's-eye view.

Part III

Formatting Documents and Text

Half the work in word processing is getting the text to look good on the page. "Appearances are everything," Oscar Wilde once remarked. The appearance of your documents should make as good an impression as their words, and that is what Part III is all about.

In this part . . .

✔ Changing the look of text

✔ Using styles, the Format Painter, and other techniques to format text quickly

✔ Creating and formatting tables

✔ Changing page margins, indentations, and tab settings

✔ Numbering lines and headings

Adding Bold, Italic, Underline, and Other Effects

Embellishing text with **boldface,** *italics,* underline, and other font styles and text effects is easy. You can do it with the Formatting toolbar or by way of the Format➪Font command. First the Formatting toolbar:

B

+ **Boldface:** Click the Bold button (or press Ctrl+B) and start typing. If you've already entered the text, select the text first and then click Bold or press Ctrl+B. Bold text is often used in headings.

I

+ **Italics:** Click the Italic button (or press Ctrl+I). Select the text first if you've already entered it. Italics are used to show emphasis and also for foreign words such as *voilà, gung hay fat choy,* and *Que magnifico!*

U

+ **Underline:** Click the Underline button (or press Ctrl+U). Select the text first and then click the button if you've already typed the text. You can also get double underlines with the Format➪Font command.

The second way to get boldface, italicized, and underline text is to choose Format➪Font or right-click text and choose Font from the shortcut menu. When the Font dialog box appears, choose options from the Font Style scroll list.

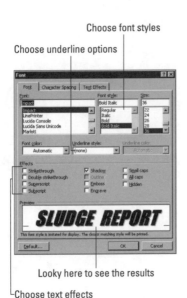

Choose font styles

Choose underline options

Looky here to see the results

Choose text effects

The Font dialog box offers many other options for embellishing text. They are shown in the following illustration. By choosing combinations of font styles and text effects, you can create interesting but sometimes unreadable letters and words.

Underline	Word offers no less than 17 different ways to underline words and letters.
Strikethrough	Lawyers use the Strikethrough style to show where text has been struck from legal contracts.
Double Strikethrough	Egotistical lawyers, if there are any, use the Double Strikethrough style.
Superscript	Used to mark footnotes in text, in math and scientific formulas, and in ordinal numbers (1st, 2nd, 3rd, and so on).
Subscript	Used in math and chemistry equations (H_2O).
Shadow	MAKES LETTERS APPEAR TO CAST A SHADOW.
Emboss	MAKES THE LETTERS APPEAR TO STAND UP FROM THE PAPER.
Outline	MAKES THE LETTERS APPEAR IN OUTLINE FORM.
Engrave	GIVES THE IMPRESSION THAT THE LETTERS WERE CHISELED IN STONE.
Small Caps	Used for time designations ("Columbus arrived in America on October 9 in A.D. 1492 at 11:30 A.M."). Not all fonts can produce small capital letters.
All Caps	YOU KNOW WHAT THIS DOES, I TRUST.
Hidden	Keeps text from being printed or displayed (see "Hidden Text and Secret Messages" in Part VII).

It's easy to overdo it with text effects. Use them sparingly. When it comes to text effects, a little goes a long way.

Applying Styles for Consistent Formatting

If you want to do any serious work whatsoever in Word 2000, you need to know about styles. A *style* is a collection of formats that have been bundled under one name. Instead of visiting many different dialog boxes to reformat a paragraph, you can choose a style from the Style menu — and the paragraph is reformatted instantaneously. If you modify a style, Word instantly modifies all paragraphs in your document that were assigned the given style.

What's more, many Word features rely on styles. For example, before you can see the Document Map, organize a document with an outline, or generate a table of contents, you must have assigned heading styles to the headings in your document. Turning a Word document into a Web page is easy if you thoughtfully assigned styles to the different parts of the document.

By using styles, you make sure that the different parts of a document are consistent with one another and that your document has a professional look.

Applying a style to text and paragraphs

Open the Style menu on the Formatting toolbar to see which styles are available in the document you are working on. A simple document created by clicking the New Blank Document button or pressing Ctrl+N has but a few basic styles, but documents like the one shown here that were created with a template come with many styles.

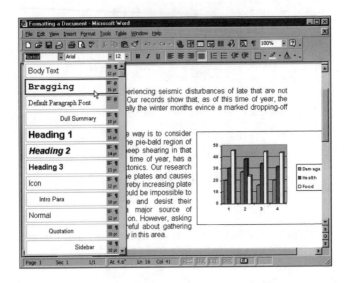

To tell which style has been assigned to a paragraph, click the paragraph and glance at the style name in the Style drop-down list. Names on the Style drop-down list give a hint of what the styles do to paragraphs and text. Pull down the Style drop-down list to see what I mean. Each name is formatted to look like a style, and the box to the right of each name tells how the style aligns text, the font size of the text, and whether the style is a paragraph or character style. *Paragraph styles,* which are marked by the paragraph symbol on the Style drop-down list, determine the formatting of entire paragraphs. Create and use *character styles* as a means of changing fonts and type sizes quickly in Word. Character styles are marked with an underlined *a*.

By now you must be itching to apply a style. Follow these steps:

1. Click the paragraph you want to apply the style to, or, to apply a style to several paragraphs, select all or part of them. If you're applying a character style, select the letters whose formatting you want to change.

2. Click the down arrow on the Style drop-down list to see the list of styles.

3. Click a style name.

You can also take the long way around by choosing Format⇨Style, choosing a style from the Styles list in the Style dialog box, and clicking Apply.

In a document to which a lot of styles have been applied, it is sometimes hard to tell which style is which. To make that easier, choose Tools⇨Options, click the View tab in the Options dialog box, click the up arrow in the Style Area Width box a few times, and click OK. Back in your document, you see the names of the styles you applied on the left side of your screen. You can also print examples of all styles used in a document by choosing File⇨Print to open the Print dialog box, choosing Styles from the Print What drop-down list, and clicking OK.

Creating a new style

You can create new styles and add them to the Style menu in two ways: directly from the screen or with the Format⇨Style command. First, the directly-from-the-screen method, which you can use to create paragraph styles.

1. Click a paragraph whose formatting you would like to turn into a style and apply to other paragraphs in your document. Remember, a heading is also a paragraph as far as Word is concerned, so if you're creating a style for a heading, click the heading.

2. Click in the Style drop-down list and type a name for the style. Choose a meaningful name that you will remember.

3. Press the Enter key.

When you create a new style from scratch with the Format⇨Style command, it takes a bit longer, but you can be very precise about the style and its formatting.

1. Choose Format⇨Style.

2. Click the New button in the Style dialog box.

3. Fill in the New Style dialog box. As you do so, keep your eyes on the Preview box. It shows you what your new style will look like in a document.

- **Name:** Enter a name for the style. The name you enter will appear on the Style menu.

- **Style Type:** Click the down arrow and choose Character if you're creating a style for characters rather than paragraphs. If you often use an exotic combination of a font and boldfacing, for example, you can create a style for it and simply click the style name on the Style menu instead of going to the trouble of formatting the characters in the document.

- **Based On:** If your new style is similar to one that is already on the menu, click here and choose the style to get a head start on creating the new one. Be warned, however, that if you or someone else changes the Based On style, your new style will inherit those changes and be altered as well.

- **Style for Following Paragraph:** Choose a style from the drop-down list if the style you're creating is always followed by an existing style. For example, a new style called "Chapter Title" might always be followed by a style called "Chapter Intro Paragraph." If that were the case, you would choose "Chapter Intro Paragraph" from this drop-down list.

- **Add to Template:** Adds the style to the document's template so that other documents based on the template you are using can also make use of the new style.

- **Automatically Update:** Normally when you make a formatting change to a paragraph, the style assigned to the paragraph does not change at all, but the style does change if you check this box. By checking this box, you tell Word to alter the style itself each time you alter a paragraph to which you've assigned the style. With this box checked, all paragraphs in the document that were assigned the style are altered each time you change a single paragraph that was assigned the style.

- **Format:** This is the important one. Click the button and make a formatting choice. Word takes you to dialog boxes so that you can create the style.

- **Shortcut Key:** Opens a dialog box so that you can apply the new style simply by pressing a shortcut key combination.

4. Click OK to close the New Style dialog box.

5. Click Apply to format the paragraph.

Modifying a style

What if you decide at the end of an 80-page document that all 35 introductory paragraphs to which you've assigned the "Intro Para" style look funny? If you clicked the Automatically Update check box in the New Style dialog box when you created the style, all you have to do is alter a paragraph to which you assigned the Intro Para style to alter all 35 introductory paragraphs. However, if you decided against updating styles automatically, you can still change the introductory paragraphs throughout your document. Follow these steps to modify a style that isn't updated automatically:

1. Click any paragraph or group of characters to which you've assigned the style you want to change.

2. Reformat the paragraph or characters.

3. Click in the Style box on the Formatting toolbar. When you do so, you click the name of the style you are modifying.

4. Press Enter. The Modify Style dialog box appears:

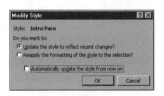

5. Click the Update the Style to Reflect Recent Changes? radio button. While you're here, you might also click the Automatically Update the Style from Now On check box to update the style automatically from now on. (If you change your mind about modifying the style, click the Reapply the Formatting of the Style to the Selection? radio button.)

6. Click OK.

If you've devised a tortuously complicated style and want to change it, use the Modify Style dialog box. Choose Format⇨Style and click the Modify button in the Style dialog box. If the Modify Style dialog box looks familiar, that's because it is identical to the New Style dialog box you used to create the style in the first place. Change the settings, click OK, and click Apply to apply the new style throughout your document.

Copying styles from different documents and templates

Suppose that you like a style in one document and you want to copy it to another so you can use it there. Copying styles between documents is easy as long as the style you want to copy doesn't have the same name as a style in the document you want to copy it to. Follow these steps to copy a style from one document to another:

1. Select a paragraph that was assigned the style you want to copy. Be sure to select the entire paragraph.

2. Choose Edit⇨Copy or press Ctrl+C to copy the paragraph to the Clipboard.

3. Switch to the document you want to copy the style to and choose Edit⇨Paste or press Ctrl+V. The style along with the text is copied to the second document.

4. Delete the text. The style remains on the Style menu even though the text is deleted.

You can always rename a style if that proves necessary to copy it elsewhere. To rename a style, choose Format⇨Style, select the style's name in the Style dialog box, click the Modify button, enter a new name in the Name text box, click OK, and click Apply.

The other way to copy styles is to use the Organizer. With the Organizer, you can copy several styles at once, and you can also copy styles between templates. Follow these steps:

1. Open the document or template you want to copy the styles from, choose Format⇨Style, and click the Organizer button in the Style dialog box. You see the Organizer dialog box. Styles in the document that you opened appear in the In box on the left side of the dialog box.

2. Click the Close File button on the right side of the dialog box. The button changes names and becomes the Open File button.

3. Click the Open File button and, in the Open dialog box, find and select the document or template to which you want to copy styles; then click the Open button.

To copy styles to a document, select Word Documents on the Files of Type drop-down list and select Document Templates to copy styles to a template. (**See also** "Opening a Document" in Part II if you need help negotiating the Open dialog box.)

4. In the Organizer dialog box, Ctrl+click the names of styles on the left side of the dialog box to copy the styles to the document or template listed on the right side of the dialog box. As you click the names, they are highlighted.

Ctrl+click the styles you want to copy

Click the copy button

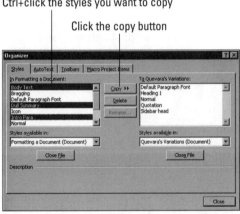

5. Click the Copy button. The names of styles that you copied appear on the right side of the Organizer dialog box.

6. Click the Close button.

7. Click Yes when Word asks if you want to save the new styles in the document to which you copied them.

Centering, Justifying, and Aligning Text

All you have to do to align text in a new way is select the text and either click an Alignment button on the Formatting toolbar or press a keyboard shortcut:

Button	Button Name	Keyboard Shortcut	What It Does
≡	Align Left	Ctrl+L	Lines up text along the left margin or left side of columns.
≡	Center	Ctrl+E	Centers text, leaving space on both sides.
≡	Align Right	Ctrl+R	Lines up text along the right margin or right side of columns.
≡	Justify	Ctrl+J	Lines up text on both the left and right margins or sides of columns.

Unless it is in columns, text is aligned with respect to the left and right *margins,* not the left and right sides of the page. This illustration may give you a clearer idea of the alignment options:

Left-aligned text is used in most kinds of documents. It hugs the left margin. It is easiest to read. With left-aligned text, lines break unevenly on the right margin.

Headings Are Usually Center-Aligned

You don't see right-aligned text very often, but it has its uses. For example, the column on the left side of the first page of newsletters is sometimes right-aligned.

Justified text is good for formal documents and for columns where lots of text has to be squeezed into a narrow space. You get uneven spaces between words with justified text. I think justified text should be hyphenated to keep those uneven spaces to a minimum.

Changing the Font of Text

Font is the catchall name for type style and type size. When you change fonts, you choose another style of type or change the size of the letters. Word offers a whole bunch of different fonts. You can see their names by clicking the down arrow next to the Font drop-down list and scrolling down the list. Fonts with *TT* beside their names are *TrueType fonts.* These fonts look the same on-screen as they do when printed on paper.

To change the font:

1. Select the text or place the cursor where you want the font to change.

2. Click the down arrow on the Font drop-down list. You see the names of fonts, each one dressed up and looking exactly like itself. Word puts all the fonts you've used so far in the document at the top of the Font drop-down list to make it easier for you to find the fonts you use most often.

3. Scroll down the list of fonts, if necessary.

4. Click a font name.

To change the size of letters:

1. Select the letters or place the cursor where you want the larger or smaller letters to start appearing.

2. Click the down arrow on the Font Size drop-down list.

3. Scroll down the list if you want a large font.

4. Click a point size — 8, 12, 36, 48, and so on.

You can also change font sizes quickly by selecting the text and pressing Ctrl+Shift+< or Ctrl+Shift+>, or by clicking in the Font Size drop-down list, entering a point size yourself, and pressing Enter. To change fonts and fonts sizes at the same time, choose Format⇨ Font and make your choices in the Font dialog box.

Type is measured in *points*. A point is $1/72$ of an inch. The larger the point size, the larger the letters. Business and personal letters usually use 10- or 12-point type. For headings, choose a larger point size. In this book, first-level main headings are 18 points high and are set in the Cascade Script font. The text you are reading is Cheltenham 9-point font. Just thought you wanted to know.

When you open a brand-new document and start typing, does the text appear in your favorite font? If it doesn't, you can make the font you use most often the default font:

1. Choose Format⇨Font.

2. Choose the font in the dialog box.

3. Click the Default button.

4. Click Yes when Word asks you if this font really should be the default font.

Constructing the Perfect Table

As everyone who has ever worked on one knows, tables are a chore. Getting all the columns to fit, making columns and rows the right width and height, and editing the text in a table is not easy. So problematic are tables that Word has devoted an entire menu to constructing them: the Table menu. Fortunately for you, the commands on this menu make formatting and working with tables easy.

This section explains how to create tables, enter text into tables, change the number and size of columns and rows, sort tables, and format tables.

Like so much else in Computerland, tables have their own jargon. A *cell* is the box that is formed where a row and column intersect. Each cell holds one data item. The *header row* is the name of the labels along the top row that explain what is in the columns below. *Borders* are the lines in the table. The *gridlines* are the gray lines that show where the columns and rows are. Gridlines are not printed — they appear to help you format your table. (Choose Table⇨Show Gridlines or Table⇨Hide Gridlines to display or hide them.) Word prints only the borders when you print a table.

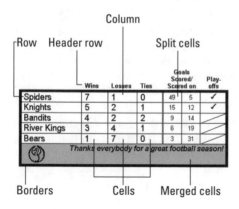

If you are having a lot of trouble making a table fit on the page, try printing it as a landscape document. *See also* "Landscape Documents," later in this part.

Creating a table

Word offers no less than four ways to create the cells and rows for a table: the Insert Table button, the Draw Table button, the Table⇨Insert⇨Table command, and the Table⇨Convert⇨Text to Table command.

The fastest way to create a table is to click the Insert Table button on the Standard toolbar:

1. Place the cursor where you want the table to go.

2. Click the Insert Table button, drag out the menu to the number of rows and columns you want, and let go of the mouse button.

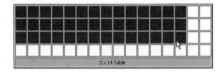

That's easy enough. Another easy way is to make like your computer is a scratch pad and draw a table. This is the way to create a table if you want rows and columns of different widths and heights. As "Merging and splitting cells and tables," a bit later in this part explains, merging and splitting cells with the Table menu commands is far more difficult than simply drawing merged and split cells.

1. To draw a table, choose Table⇨Draw Table or click the Draw Table button on the Tables and Borders toolbar. Choose a thick line from the Line Weight menu on the toolbar to see the lines better as you draw them. The pointer changes into a pencil. By the way, you can click the Tables and Borders button on the Standard toolbar to display the Tables and Border toolbar.

2. Start drawing. As you drag the pencil on-screen, you get columns and rows.

3. If you make a mistake, click the Eraser button on the Tables and Border toolbar. The pointer changes into an eraser. Drag it over the parts of the table you regret drawing.

4. When you are finished drawing the table, click the Draw Table button to put the pencil away.

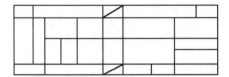

The only advantage of the Table⇨Insert⇨Table command is that it gives you the opportunity to decide how wide to make the table:

1. Place the cursor where you want the table to be.

2. Choose Table⇨Insert⇨Table. The Insert Table dialog box appears.

3. In the Number of Columns box, enter the number of columns you want.

4. In the Number of Rows box, enter the number of rows you want.

5. Under AutoFit Behavior, you can enter a measurement in the Fixed Column Width text box to make all columns the same width. (The Auto setting creates columns of equal width and stretches the table so that it fits across the page between the left and right margin.) *See also* "Resizing columns and rows," later in this part, to find out what the other two options are.

6. Click the AutoFormat button to open a dialog box from which you can choose one of Word's table formats. These formats are explained in the section "Formatting a table with Word's AutoFormats" later in this part.

7. Click OK.

The fourth way to create a table is to convert text that you've already entered. This is the way to go if you've created a list and you don't want to go to the trouble of re-entering the text all over again for the new table. To convert text into a table:

1. Either press Tab or enter a comma in the list where you want columns to be divided. For example, if you are turning an address list into a table, put each name and address on one line and press Tab or enter a comma after the first name, the last name, the street address, the city, the state, and the zip code. For this feature to work, each name and address — each line — must have the same number of tab spaces or commas in it.

2. Start a new paragraph — press Enter, that is — where you want each row to end.

3. Select the text you want to turn into a table.

4. Choose Table⇨Convert⇨Text to Table.

5. Under Separate Text At in the Convert Text to Table dialog box, choose Tabs or Commas to tell Word how the columns are separated.

6. Choose an AutoFit Behavior option, if you want. (***See also*** "Resizing columns and rows," later in this section.)

7. Click OK.

In this illustration, five tab stops were entered on each line in an address list. Below the list is the table that was created from the address list.

Roger Wilco	1227 Jersey St.	San Francisco	CA	94114	415/555-3424
Dane Bergard	2234 Pax St.	Pacifica	CA	93303	415/555-2341
J.S. Minnow	10 Taylor St.	Daly City	CA	94404	415/555-9843

Roger Wilco	1227 Jersey St.	San Francisco	CA	94114	415/555-3424
Dane Bergard	2234 Pax St.	Pacifica	CA	93303	415/555-2341
J.S. Minnow	10 Taylor St.	Daly City	CA	94404	415/555-9843

Entering text and numbers in a table

After you've created the table, you can start entering text. All you have to do is click in a cell and start typing. To help you work more quickly, here are some shortcuts for moving the cursor in a table:

Press	Moves the Cursor To
Tab	Next column in row
Shift+Tab	Previous column in row
Alt+Home	Start of row
Alt+End	End of row
↓	Row below
↑	Row above
Alt+Page Up	Top of column
Alt+Page Down	Bottom of column

If you need to add a row at the bottom of the table to enter more text, place the cursor in the last column of the last row and press the Tab key.

Changing the layout of a table

Very likely, you created too many or too few rows or columns for your table. Some columns are probably too wide, and others may be too narrow. If that is the case, you have to change the layout of the table by deleting, inserting, and changing the size of columns and rows. (Putting borders around tables and embellishing them in other ways is explained later in this entry.)

Selecting different parts of a table

Before you can fool with cells, rows, or columns, you have to select them:

+ **Cells:** To select a cell, click in it. You can select several cells at once by dragging the cursor over them.

+ **Rows:** Place the cursor in the left margin and click to select one row, or click and drag to select several rows. You can also select rows by placing the cursor in the row you want to select and then choosing the Table➪Select➪Row command. To select several rows, select cells in the rows and then choose the Table➪Select➪Row command.

+ **Columns:** To select a column, move the cursor to the top of the column. When the cursor changes into a fat down-pointing arrow, click once. You can click and drag to select several columns. The other way to select a column is to click anywhere in the column and choose Table➪Select➪Column. To select several columns with this command, select cells in the columns before giving the Select command.

+ **A table:** To select a table, click in the table and choose Table➪Select➪Table; hold down the Alt key and double-click; or press Alt+5 (the 5 on the numeric keypad, not the one on the keyboard).

Inserting and deleting columns and rows

Here's the lowdown on inserting and deleting columns and rows:

+ **Inserting columns:** To insert a blank column, select the column to the right of where you want the new column to go. If you want to insert two or more columns, select the number of columns you want to add. Then right-click and choose Insert Columns, or choose Table➪Insert➪Columns to the Left (or Columns to the Right).

✦ **Deleting columns:** To delete columns, select them. Then choose Table⇨Delete⇨Columns, or right-click and choose Delete Columns. (Pressing the Delete key deletes the data in the column.)

✦ **Inserting rows:** To insert a blank row, select the row below which you want the new one to appear. If you want to insert more than one row, select more than one. Then right-click and choose Insert Rows, or choose Table⇨Insert⇨Rows Above (or Rows Below). You can also insert a row at the end of a table by moving the cursor into the last cell in the last row and pressing Tab.

✦ **Deleting rows:** To delete rows, select them and choose Table⇨Delete⇨Rows, or right-click and choose Delete Rows from the shortcut menu. (Pressing the Delete key deletes the data in the row.)

Moving columns and rows

Because there is no elegant way to move a column or row, you should move only one at a time. If you try to move several at once, you open a can of worms that is best left unopened. To move a column or row:

1. Select the column or row you want to move.

2. Right-click in the selection and choose Cut from the shortcut menu. The column or row disappears to the Clipboard.

3. Move the column or row:

• **Column:** Click in the topmost cell in the column to the right of where you want to move the column. In other words, to make what is now column 4 column 2, cut column 4 and click in the topmost cell of column 2. Then right-click and choose Paste Columns from the shortcut menu.

• **Row:** Move the cursor into the first column of the row below which you want to move your row. In other words, if you're placing the row between what are now rows 6 and 7, put the cursor in row 7. Then right-click and choose Paste Rows from the shortcut menu.

Resizing columns and rows

The fastest way to adjust the width of columns and the height of rows is to "eyeball it." To make a column wider or narrower, move the cursor onto a gridline or border. When the cursor changes into a double-headed arrow, start dragging. Tug and pull, tug and pull until the column is the right width or the row is the right height. You can also slide the column bars on the horizontal ruler or the rows bars on the vertical ruler (if you're in Print Layout View) to change the width of columns and height of rows.

Because resizing columns and rows can be problematic, Word offers these commands on the Table⇨AutoFit submenu for adjusting the width and height of rows and columns:

> ✦ **AutoFit to Contents:** Makes each column wide enough to accommodate its widest entry.

> ✦ **AutoFit to Window:** Stretches the table so that it fits across the page between the left and right margin.

> ✦ **Fixed Column Width:** Fixes the column widths at their current settings.

> ✦ **Distribute Rows Evenly:** Makes all rows the same height as the tallest row. You can also click the Distribute Rows Evenly button on the Tables and Borders toolbar. Select rows before giving this command to make the command affect only the rows you selected.

> ✦ **Distribute Columns Evenly:** Makes all columns the same width. You can also click the Distribute Columns Evenly button. Select columns before giving this command if you want to change the size of a few rows, not all the rows in the table.

Yet another technique for adjusting row heights and columns widths is to choose Table⇨Table Properties and visit the Row and Column tabs in the Table Properties dialog box. There, you can enter specific measurements for row heights and column widths. Click the Previous or Next button to go from row to row or column to column. This technique isn't nearly as useful as the others, however, because the Table Properties dialog box doesn't have a Preview box and you can't see what your choices do to the table.

Aligning text in columns and rows

The easiest way to align text in the columns or cells is to rely on the Align Left, Center, Align Right, and Justify buttons on the Standard toolbar. Select a cell, a column, or columns and click one of those buttons to align the text in a column the same way.

However, if you want to get really fancy, you can align text by clicking an Align button on the Tables and Borders toolbar. Select the cells that need aligning, click the down arrow beside the Align button, and click one of the nine buttons to align text in a new way:

Sorting, or reordering, a table

The fastest way to rearrange the rows in a table is to use the Table⇨Sort command or click one of the Sort buttons on the Tables and Borders toolbar. *Sorting* means to rearrange all the rows in a table on the basis of data in one column. For example, the first table shown here is arranged, or sorted, on the fifth column, "Total Votes." This column has been sorted in *descending* order from most to fewest votes. The second table has been sorted on the first column. It is sorted by the candidates' names in *ascending* order alphabetically. Both tables present the same information, but the information has been sorted in different ways.

	1st Ward	2nd Ward	3rd Ward	Total Votes
Muñoz	2,567	7,399	10,420	20,386
Wilson	3,113	9,907	4,872	17,892
Teel	67	211	89	367
Greenstein	12	2	113	127

	1st Ward	2nd Ward	3rd Ward	Total Votes
Greenstein	12	2	113	127
Muñoz	2,567	7,399	10,420	20,386
Teel	67	211	89	367
Wilson	3,113	9,907	4,872	17,892

The difference between ascending and descending sorts is as follows:

 ✦ Ascending arranges text from A to Z, numbers from smallest to largest, and dates from the oldest in time to the most recent.

 ✦ Descending arranges text from Z to A, numbers from largest to smallest, and dates from most recent to the oldest in time.

When you rearrange a table by sorting it, Word rearranges the formatting as well as the data. Do your sorting before you format the table.

For simple sorts, select the column that is to be the basis of the sort and click the Sort Descending button on the Tables and Borders toolbar for a descending sort or the Sort Ascending button for an ascending sort. You can also select a column and choose Table⇔Sort, click the Ascending or Descending radio button in the Sort dialog box, and click OK.

Dressing up your table

After you enter the text, put the rows and columns in place, and make them the right size, the fun begins. Now you can dress up your table and make it look snazzy.

Almost everything you can do to a document you can do to a table by selecting parts of it and choosing menu commands or clicking buttons. You can change text fonts, align data in the cells in different ways, and even import a graphic into a cell. You can also play with the borders that divide the rows and columns and "shade" columns, rows, and cells by filling them with gray shades or a black background. Read on to find out how to do these tricks and also how to center a table or align it with the right page margin.

Formatting a table with Word's AutoFormats

The fastest way to get a good-looking table is to let Word do the work for you:

1. Click your table.

2. Choose Table⇔Table AutoFormat. The Table AutoFormat dialog box appears:

Watch this box!

3. Rummage through the Formats menu until you find a table to your liking. You can see what tables look like in the Preview box.

4. Check and uncheck the Formats to Apply and Apply Special Formats To check boxes. As you do so, watch the Preview box to see what your choices do.

5. When you have the right table format, click OK.

Getting your own borders, shading, and color

Instead of relying on Word's Table⇨Table AutoFormat command, you can draw borders yourself and shade or give color to different parts of a table as well. Doing so by means of the Tables and Borders toolbar is easier than you might think.

Line weight menu ┌Border Color button

Line Style menu │ │ Shading Color button and menu

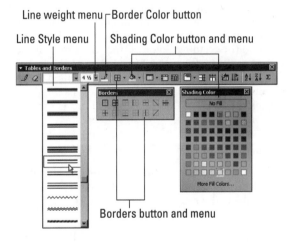

Borders button and menu

Click the Tables and Borders button on the Standard toolbar to display the Tables and Borders toolbar and then follow these steps to decorate a table with borders, shading, and color:

1. Select the part of the table that you want to decorate. For example, to put a border along the top or bottom of a row, select the row; to shade two columns, select them.

2. Use the tools on the Tables and Borders toolbar to decorate your table:

- **Choosing lines for borders:** Click the down arrow beside the Line Style button and choose a line, dashed line, double line, or wiggly line for the border. (Choose No Border if you don't want a border or you are removing one that is already there.) Then click the down arrow beside the Line Weight button to choose a line width for the border.

- **Choosing line colors:** Click the Border Color button and click one of the color boxes on the menu. Use the Automatic choice to remove colors and gray shades.

- **Drawing the border lines:** Click the down arrow beside the Border button and choose one of the border buttons on the menu. (Click No Border to remove borders.) For example, click the Top Border button to put a border along the top of the part of the table you selected in Step 1; click the Inside Border button to put the border on the interior lines of the part of the table you selected.

- **Shading or giving a color background to table cells:** Click the down arrow on the Shading Color menu and click one of the color or gray-shade buttons.

After you make a choice from a menu on the Tables and Borders toolbar, the choice you make appears on the button that is used to open the menu. Choose Blue on the Shading Color menu, for example, and the Shading Color button turns blue. If the choice you want to make from a menu happens to be the last choice you made, you can click the button instead of opening the menu. To make a blue background show in a table, for example, you can simply click the Shading Color button as long as the Shading Color button is blue.

Putting a table in the middle or side of the page

As long as a table doesn't fill the page, you can lean it against the left or right margin or put it squarely between the margins. You can even make text wrap around the table. Follow these steps to do so:

1. Click the table and choose Table➪Table Properties.

2. Click the Table tab in the Table Properties dialog box, if necessary.

3. Choose an Alignment option — Left, Center, or Right. If you choose Left, you can enter a measurement in the Indent from Left box to indent the table from the left margin.

4. If you want text to wrap around the side of your table, click the Around option. (*See also* "Handling Objects on the Page" in Part VI to learn more about wrapping.)

5. Click OK.

Repeating header rows on subsequent pages

Making sure that the header row appears on a new page if the table breaks across pages is absolutely essential. Without a header row, readers can't tell what the information in a table is or means. To make the header row (or rows) repeat on the top of each new page, place the cursor in the header row (or select the header rows if you have more than one) and choose Table⇨Heading Rows Repeat. By the way, heading rows appear only in Print Layout view, so don't worry if you're in Normal view and you can't see them.

Merging and splitting cells and tables

The cells in the second row in the following table have been merged to create one large cell. Where the first and third row have six cells, the second has only one:

1993	1994	1995	1996	1997	1998
Sammy Sosa's Homeruns					
19	27	44	39	53	64

To merge cells in a table:

1. Select the cells you want to merge.

2. Choose Table⇨Merge Cells or click the Merge Cells button on the Tables and Borders toolbar.

In the same vein, you can split a cell into two or more cells:

1. Click in the cell you want to split.

2. Choose Table⇨Split Cells or click the Split Cells button on the Tables and Borders toolbars.

3. In the Split Cells dialog box, declare how many cells you want to split the cell into and click OK.

Still in the same vein, you can split a table as well:

1. Place the cursor in what you want to be the first row of the new table.

2. Choose Table⇨Split Table.

Using math formulas in tables

No, you don't have to add the figures in columns and rows yourself; Word gladly does that for you. Word can perform other mathematical calculations as well.

To total the figures in a column or row, place the cursor in the cell that is to hold the total and click the AutoSum button on the Tables and Borders toolbar.

The AutoSum button, however, is only good for adding figures. To perform other mathematical calculations and tell Word how to format sums and products:

1. Put the cursor in the cell that will hold the sum or product of the cells above, below, to the right, or to the left.

2. Choose Table⇨Formula. The Formula dialog box appears:

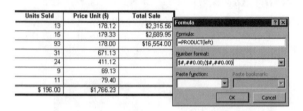

3. In its wisdom, Word makes a very educated guess about what you want the formula to do and places a formula in the Formula box. If this isn't the formula you want, delete everything except the equal sign in the Formula box, click the down arrow in the Paste Function box, and choose another formula. You may have to type **left, right, above,** or **below** in the parentheses beside the formula to tell Word where the figures that you want it to compute are.

4. In the Number Format box, click the down arrow and choose a format for your number.

5. Click OK.

Word does not calculate blank cells in formulas. Enter a **0** in blank cells if you want them to be included in calculations. You can copy functions from one cell to another to save yourself the trouble of opening the Formula dialog box.

Creating Numbered and Bulleted Lists

Numbered lists are invaluable in manuals and books like this one that present a lot of step-by-step procedures. Use bulleted lists when you want to present alternatives to the reader. A *bullet* is a black filled-in circle or other character.

Simple numbered and bulleted lists

The fastest, cleanest, and most honest way to create a numbered or bulleted list is to enter the text without any concern for numbers or bullets. Just press Enter at the end of each step or bulleted entry. When you're done, select the list and click the Numbering or Bullets button on the Formatting toolbar.

Another way to create a numbered list is to type the number 1, type a period, press the spacebar, type the first entry in the list, and press Enter to get to the next line and type the second entry. As soon as you press Enter, Word inserts the number 2 and formats the list for you. Keep typing list entries, and Word keeps right on numbering and formatting the list. *To end this list, press ENTER twice.*

Ending and continuing lists

To end a numbered or bulleted list and tell Word that you want to go back to writing normal paragraphs, go to the Bullets and Numbering dialog box either by choosing Format⇨Bullets and Numbering or by right-clicking and choosing Bullets and Numbering from the shortcut menu. In the dialog box, click the Numbered or Bulleted tab (if necessary), select None, and then click OK.

Suppose that you want a numbered list to pick up where a list you entered earlier ended. In other words, suppose that you ended a four-step list a couple of paragraphs back and now you want the list to resume at Step 5. In that case, click the Numbering button to start numbering again, open the Bullets and Numbering dialog box, and click the Continue Previous List option button. The list will pick up where the previous numbered list in the document left off.

Also in the Bullets and Numbering dialog box is an option for starting a list anew. Choose Restart Numbering when Word insists on starting a list with a number other than 1 or when you want to break off one list and start another.

Constructing lists of your own

If you are an individualist and you want numbered and bulleted lists to work your way, start from the Bullets and Numbering dialog box. (Choose Format⇨Bullets and Numbering to get there.) On the Bulleted and Numbered tabs, you can choose among different kinds of bullets and different numbering schemes.

If those choices aren't good enough for you, click the Customize button to open the Customize Numbered List or Customize Bulleted List dialog box. These dialog boxes offer opportunities for indenting numbers or bullets and the text that follows them in new ways. You can also choose fonts for the numbers and symbols for the bullets. Be sure to watch the Preview area of these dialog boxes. It shows exactly what you are doing to your bulleted or numbered lists.

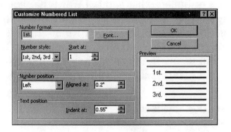

Dividing a Document into Sections

Every document has at least one *section*. That's why "Sec 1" appears on the left side of the status bar at the bottom of the screen. When you want to change page numbering schemes, headers and footers, margin sizes, and page layouts, you have to create a section break to start a new section. Word creates one for you when you create newspaper-style columns or change the size of margins. To create a new section:

1. Click where you want to insert a section break.

2. Choose Insert⇨Break.

3. Under Section Break Types, tell Word which kind of section break you want. All four section break options create a new section, but they do so in different ways:

- **Next Page:** Inserts a page break as well as a section break so that the new section can start at the top of a new page (the next one). Select this option to start a new chapter, for example.

- **Continuous:** Inserts a section break in the middle of a page. Select this option, for example, if you want to introduce newspaper-style columns in the middle of a page.

- **Even Page:** Starts the new section on the next even page. This option is good for two-sided documents where the headers on the left- and right-hand pages are different.

- **Odd Page:** Starts the new section on the next odd page. You might choose this option if you have a book in which chapters start on odd pages. (By convention, that's where they start.)

4. Click OK.

In Normal View, you can tell where a section ends because `Section Break` and a double dotted line appear on-screen. The only way to tell where a section ends in Print Layout View is to glance at the "Sec" listing on the status bar or click the Show/Hide ¶ button. To delete a section break, make sure that you are in Normal View, click the dotted line, and press the Delete key.

Fast Formatting with the Format Painter

The fastest way to format a document is with the Format Painter. You can use this tool to make sure that the headings, lists, text paragraphs, and whatnot in your document are formatted the same way. To use the Format Painter, follow these steps:

1. Click on the text whose formats you want to apply throughout your document. For example, if your document is a report with first-, second-, and third-level heads, format a first-level head so that it looks just right and click it.

2. Double-click the Format Painter button. The mouse pointer changes into a paint brush icon.

3. Find the text you want to copy the format to, click the mouse button, and roll the mouse pointer over it as though you were selecting it. When you're done, the text takes on the new formats.

4. Keep going. Find every place in your document that you can copy this format to and baste it with the Format Painter. You can click the scroll bar and use keyboard commands to move through your document.

5. Click the Format Painter button when you're done.

Indenting Paragraphs and First Lines

An *indent* is the distance between a margin and the text, not the left side of the page and the text. Word offers a handful of different ways to change the indentation of paragraphs.

The fastest way is to use the Increase Indent and Decrease Indent buttons on the Formatting toolbar to move the paragraph away from or toward the left margin:

1. Click in the paragraph whose indentation you want to change. If you want to change more than one paragraph, select them.

2. Click one of these buttons as many times as necessary to indent the text:

  • **Increase Indent:** Indents the paragraph from the left margin by one tab stop. (You can also press Ctrl+M.)

  • **Decrease Indent:** Moves the paragraph back toward the left margin by one tab stop. (You can also press Ctrl+Shift+M.)

You can also change indentations by using the ruler to "eyeball it." This technique requires some dexterity with the mouse, but it allows you to see precisely where paragraphs and the first lines of paragraphs are indented.

1. Choose View⇨Ruler, if necessary, to put the ruler on-screen.

2. Select the paragraph or paragraphs whose indentation you want to change.

3. Slide the indent markers with the mouse:

  • **First-line indent marker:** Drag the down-pointing arrow on the ruler to indent the first line of the paragraph only.

  • **Left indent marker:** This one, on the bottom-left side of the ruler, comes in two parts. Drag the arrow that points up (called the hanging indent marker), but not the box underneath it, to move the left margin independently of the first-line indentation. To move the left indentation *and* the first-line indentation relative to the left margin, slide the box. Doing so moves everything on the left side of the ruler.

• **Right indent marker:** Drag this one to move the right side of the paragraph away from the right margin.

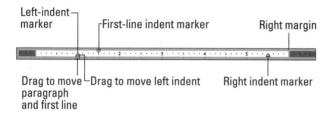

Left-indent marker

First-line indent marker

Right margin

Drag to move paragraph and first line

Drag to move left indent

Right indent marker

If you're not one for "eyeballing it," you can use the Format⇨Paragraph command to indent paragraphs:

1. Choose Format⇨Paragraph or double-click the Left or Right indent marker on the ruler.

2. Make your selections in the Indentation area.

3. Click OK.

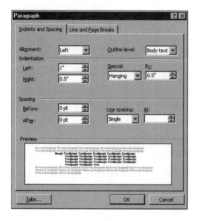

The Indentation options are self-explanatory. As you experiment, watch the Preview box — it shows exactly what your choices will do to the paragraph. In the Special drop-down list, you can choose First Line to indent the first line from the left margin or Hanging to create a *hanging indent,* an indent in which the second and subsequent lines in the paragraph are indented farther from the left margin than the first line. Enter a measurement in the By box to say how far you want these indents to travel. Did you notice the Alignment drop-down list in the upper-left corner? You can even align paragraphs from this dialog box.

Numbering the Headings in a Document

In scholarly papers and formal documents, the headings are sometimes numbered so that cross-references and commentary can refer to them by number as well as by name. The Format⇨ Bullets and Numbering command makes numbering the headings in a document very easy. The beauty of this command is that Word renumbers the headings automatically if you remove a heading or add a new one.

To use the Format⇨Bullets and Numbering command, you must have assigned heading styles to your document. (*See also* "Applying Styles for Consistent Formatting," earlier in this part.) First-level heads are given top billing in the numbering scheme. Sub-headings get lower billing.

To number the headings in a document:

1. Switch to Outline view by clicking the Outline View button in the lower-left corner of the screen or choosing View⇨Outline.

2. Click a Show Heading button (1 through 7) so that you can see only the headings in Outline view. ("Outlines for Organizing Your Work" in Part V explains Outline view.)

3. Select the headings you want to number.

4. Choose Format⇨Bullets and Numbering.

5. Click the Outline Numbered tab in the Bullets and Numbering dialog box.

6. Click a numbering scheme in the Outline Numbered tab. Notice that some choices place words as well as numbers or letters before headings.

7. Click the Cus_t_omize button if you want to devise your own numbering scheme or put a word before all headings. You can even choose new fonts for headings. If you experiment, be sure to watch the Preview box to see what kind of damage you're doing. Click OK when you're done experimenting.

8. Click OK to close the Bullets and Numbering dialog box.

If you regret having numbered the headings in your document, choose _E_dit⇨_U_ndo Bullets and Numbering (or press Ctrl+Z), or go back to the Outline Numbered tab and choose None.

Numbering the Lines in a Document

As every legal secretary and lawyer knows, the lines in a legal contract have to be numbered. You can number lines very easily with Word. The numbers appear in the margin.

1. If you want to number the lines in one section only, place the cursor in that section. To number lines starting at one place, put the cursor where you want to start numbering. To number all the lines in the document, it doesn't matter where you place the cursor.

2. Choose _F_ile⇨Page Set_u_p.

3. In the Page Setup dialog box, click the _L_ayout tab.

4. Click the Line _N_umbers button.

5. In the Line Numbers dialog box, click the Add _L_ine Numbering check box.

6. Choose options from the Line Numbers dialog box:

- **Start _A_t:** Enter the number to begin counting with if you want to begin with a number other than 1.

- **From _T_ext:** Determines how far the numbers are from the text. The larger the number you enter, the closer the numbers appear to the left side of the page.

• **Count By:** All lines are numbered, but by choosing a number here, you can make numbers appear at intervals. For example, entering **5** makes intervals of five (5, 10, 15, and so on) appear in the margin.

• **Numbering:** In legal contracts, the numbers begin anew on each page, but you can start numbering at each section or number all lines in the document consecutively.

7. Click OK.

8. Back on the Layout tab of the Page Setup dialog box, choose an Apply To option from the drop-down list. If you're numbering only a section, choose This Section. Otherwise, choose Whole Document to number all the lines or This Point Forward to number lines starting at the cursor.

9. Click OK.

To remove line numbers, follow Steps 1 through 5 of the preceding set of instructions, but this time remove the check mark from the Add Line Numbering check box. Then click OK and click OK again in the Page Setup dialog box.

You can see line numbers only in Print Layout View. Even at that, you may have to scroll to the left with the scroll bar along the bottom of the screen to see them.

Setting Up and Changing the Margins

Margins are the empty spaces along the left, right, top, and bottom sides of a page. Headers and footers are printed in the top and bottom margins, respectively.

Don't confuse margins with indents. Text is indented from the margin, not from the edge of the page. If you want to change how far a paragraph is indented, use the ruler or the Format⇨Paragraph command and change its indentation.

To change the margin settings:

1. Place the cursor where you want to change margins if you are changing margins in the middle of a document. Otherwise, to change the margins in the entire document, it doesn't matter where you place the cursor.

2. Choose File⇨Page Setup.

3. Choose the settings on the <u>M</u>argins tab and watch the Preview box to see what your choices do:

- **<u>T</u>op, <u>B</u>ottom, Le<u>f</u>t, <u>R</u>ight, I<u>n</u>side, <u>O</u>utside:** Set the top, bottom, left and right, or inside and outside, margins. (You see the I<u>n</u>side and <u>O</u>utside settings if you click the M<u>i</u>rror Margins check box.)

- **G<u>u</u>tter:** Allows extra space on the inside margin for documents that will be bound. Click the up arrow to see what binding looks like as it eats into the left side of the page and alters the left margin.

- **H<u>e</u>ader:** Increases or decreases the amount of space allowed for headers at the top of the page.

- **Footer:** Increases or decreases the amount of space allowed for footers.

- **Appl<u>y</u> To:** Choose Whole Document to apply your settings to the entire document, This Section to apply them to a section, or This Point Forward to change margins for the rest of a document. When you choose This Point Forward, Word creates a new section.

- **M<u>i</u>rror Margins:** Click this check box if you want to print on both sides of the paper and you intend to bind your document. That way, you can set the inside margin, the margin on sides of pages where the binding is, and the outside margin, the margin on the sides of pages that is not affected by binding.

- **<u>2</u> Pages Per Sheet:** For printing pamphlets and other types of documents in which the pages are half the usual size and are cut in half after printing. When you click this check box, the <u>T</u>op margin becomes the <u>O</u>utside margin, the area in the middle of the page that may need to be larger so the page can be cut, and the <u>B</u>ottom margin becomes the I<u>n</u>side margin, the area away from the dividing line that doesn't have to be as large.

- **Gutter Position:** Click the T<u>o</u>p option button if you intend to bind documents from the top, not the left side of pages.

4. Click OK.

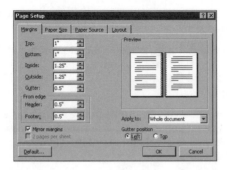

You can change the top and bottom margins with the horizontal ruler in Print Layout View. Simply drag the margin bar up or down.

If you don't care for Word's default margin settings, make your own in the Page Setup dialog box and click the Default button. Henceforth, new documents that you open will have *your* margin settings.

Working with the Ruler

The ruler along the top of the screen is there to help you change and identify margins, tab settings, and indents, as well as place graphics and text boxes. (If you don't see it, choose View⇨Ruler.) In Print Layout View, there is a similar ruler along the left side of the screen.

You can change the unit of measurement that is shown on the rulers. Choose Tools⇨Options, click the General tab, and choose Inches, Centimeters, Millimeters, Points, or Picas from the Measurement Units drop-down list. Here is what the horizontal ruler looks like with point measurements:

See also "Indenting Paragraphs and First Lines," "Setting Up and Changing the Margins," and "Working with Tabs" in this part to find out how to do those things with the rulers.

Working with Tabs

A *tab stop* is a point on the ruler around which or against which text is formatted. When you press the Tab key, you advance the text cursor by one tab stop. Tab stops are set at half-inch intervals on the ruler, but you can change that if you want to.

You can also change the type of tab. By default, tabs are left-aligned, which means that when you enter letters after you press the Tab key, the letters move toward the right in the same way that they move toward the right when text is left-aligned. However, Word also offers right, center, decimal, and bar tabs. The following illustration shows the differences between the tab settings. Notice the symbols on the ruler — they tell you what type of tab you are dealing with.

Left	Center	Right	Decimal
January	January	January	January
Oct.	Oct.	Oct.	Oct.
1234	1234	1234	1234
$45.95	$45.95	$45.95	$45.95
13,579.32	13,579.32	13,579.32	13,579.32

Tabs are a throwback to the days of the typewriter, when it was necessary to make tab stops in order to align text. Except for making leaders, everything you can do with tabs can also be done by creating a table — and it can be done far faster. All you have to do is align the text inside the table and then remove the table borders. *See also* "Constructing the Perfect Table," earlier in this part.

To change tabs or change where tabs appear on the ruler:

1. Click in the box on the left side of the ruler to get different tab settings. As you click, the symbols change, as shown:

Symbol	Tab Type
∟	Left-aligned tab
⊥	Center-aligned tab
⌐	Right-aligned tab
⊥	Decimal tab
❘	Bar tab

Left-aligned tab

Center-aligned tab

Right-aligned tab

Decimal tab   Bar tab

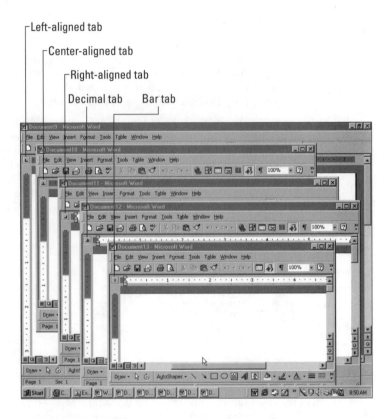

2. When you come to the symbol that represents the type of tab you want (keep clicking), click at the place on the ruler where you want to put a tab stop. You can click as many times as you want and enter more than one kind of tab.

You can move a tab on the ruler simply by dragging it to a new location. Text that has been aligned with the tab moves as well, if you select it first. To remove a tab, drag it off the ruler. When you remove a tab, the text to which it was aligned is aligned to the next tab stop on the ruler.

You can also make tab settings with the Tabs dialog box:

1. Place the cursor where you want your new tab settings to take effect. Or else select the text to which you want to apply your new tabs.

2. Choose Format⇨Tabs. You see the Tabs dialog box.

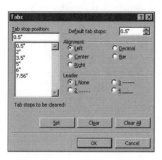

3. Enter a position for the first new tab in the Tab Stop Position box.

4. Choose an Alignment option. The Bar option places a vertical bar, or straight line, at the tab stop position. You can place numbers inside the bar tabs, for example, to help line them up, although doing so is utterly ridiculous when you can do that far more easily in a table. My personal opinion is that Microsoft invented this tab solely to be able to call it a "bar tab." Perhaps the inventor ran up a large bar tab somewhere and wanted to commemorate the event.

5. Choose a leader, if you want one. For example, if you choose 2, Word places periods in the document whenever you press Tab at this setting. A *leader* is a series of identical characters. Leaders are often found in tables of contents — they are the periods between the table of contents entry and the page number it refers to.

6. Click the Set button.

7. Repeat Steps 3 through 6 for the next tab setting and all other tab settings. If you change your mind about a setting, select it in the Tab Stop Position scroll box and click Clear. Click Clear All if you change your mind in a big way and want to start all over.

8. Click OK.

Sometimes it is hard to tell where tabs were put in the text. To find out, click the Show/Hide ¶ button to see the formatting characters, including the arrows that show where the Tab key was pressed:

```
Roger·Wilco   →  1227·Jersey·St. →  San·Francisco →  CA  →  94114  →  415/555-3424¶
Dane·Bergard →  2234·Pax·St.    →  Pacifica      →  CA  →  93303  →  415/555-2341¶
·J.S.·Minnow →  10·Taylor·St.   →  Daly·City     →      CA  →  94404  →  415/555-9843¶
```

Leaders are very elegant. For this illustration, I used left-aligned
tab stops for the characters' names and right-aligned tab stops for
the players' names. I included leaders so you can tell precisely
who played whom.

The Players

Romeo..McGeorge Wright
Juliet...................................Gabriela Hernandez
Mercutio ....Chris Suzuki
Lady Capulet...........................Mimi Hornstein

Printing Your Documents

What is a document until you print it? Not much. It's like an idea that hasn't been written down or communicated to anyone yet. A document isn't worth much until you run it through the printer and put it on paper so that other people can read it.

Part IV explains how to print documents in Word 2000. It describes how to print labels and addresses on envelopes, print on sheets of paper other than the standard 8.5 x 11, and set up the pages for printing. This part also tells you what to do if you just can't get your documents to print.

In this part . . .

✐ **Telling Word how to print documents**

✐ **Seeing what you print before you print it**

✐ **Printing envelopes and address labels**

✐ **Printing on legal-size and odd-shaped paper**

✐ **Printing thumbnail pages**

✐ **Solving problems with the printer**

Introducing Word to Your Printer

Before you can print a document, Word has to know where the paper is and what kind of printer you're using. Windows probably told its cousin Word what kind of printer you have when you installed your printer, but it doesn't hurt to check. And if you keep different paper in different trays, you need to tell Word where the right size paper is.

1. Choose File⇨Print or press Ctrl+P.

2. In the Print dialog box, click the down-arrow on the Name drop-down list and choose a printer, if necessary.

3. Click the Properties button.

4. On the Paper tab of the Properties dialog box, choose which size paper you're using or, if you're printing an envelope, which size envelope you intend to print on.

5. From the Paper Source drop-down list, choose the right tray, or choose a method of feeding envelopes to your printer if you're printing an envelope.

6. Click OK to get back to the Print dialog box, and click OK again.

You can change a printer's default settings and spare yourself the trouble of always having to choose options in the Print dialog box each time, for example, you print a legal document on legal-size paper. Click the Start button and choose Settings⇨Printers. Then, in the Printers folder, right-click the printer that you use and choose Properties. On the Paper tab in the Properties dialog box, select a new Paper Size option and click OK. Just be sure to tell your colleagues in the law office that you changed the default settings — and tell them how to change the settings back, in case someone wants to do that.

Previewing What You Print

Before you print a document, do yourself a big favor by *previewing* it. That way, you can catch errors before you send it through the printer and waste 1, 2, 5, or 20 sheets of paper. For that matter, preview your documents from time to time to make sure that they are laid out correctly.

To preview a document:

1. Put the document you're about to print on-screen.

2. Choose File⇨Print Preview or click the Print Preview button on the toolbar. A panoramic picture of your document appears on the Preview screen:

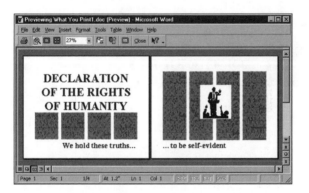

3. Use the buttons and scroll bar on the Preview screen to get a better look at your document:

- Click part of the document to zoom in and examine closely. The pointer, which previously looked like a magnifying glass with a plus sign in it, now has a minus sign where the plus sign used to be. Click again to zoom out and get back to the Preview screen. If your pointer doesn't look like a magnifying glass, click the Magnifier button on the Print Preview toolbar.

- Click the One Page or Multiple Pages button to view one or several pages at once.

- Click the Zoom Control menu and either enter a percentage and press the Enter key or choose a different percentage from the menu to see more of a page. You can also click the Page Width setting on the Zoom menu to make the page fill the Preview screen.

- Click the Shrink to Fit button, and Word shrinks your document a bit if it can. Choose this option if the last page has only a few lines of text and you want to save a piece of paper.

- The Full Screen button removes the menu bars and ruler so that you can really get the "big picture" of a page.

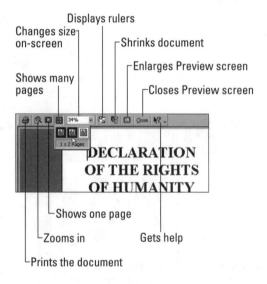

 4. Click <u>C</u>lose if you need to go back to the document and make changes; otherwise, click the Print button.

Printing Addresses on Envelopes

You don't have to address envelopes by hand, although it's often easier to do it that way. Here's how to print addresses and return addresses on envelopes:

1. Open the document that holds the letter you want to send, and select the name and address of the person you want to send the letter to.

2. Choose Tools⇨Envelopes and Labels. The Envelopes and
Labels dialog box appears with the address you selected in
the Delivery Address box. Your name and address should
appear in the Return Address box. (If it isn't there, see the Tip
at the end of this section to find out how to put it there.)

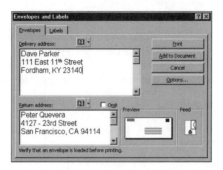

3. Change the Delivery Address or Return Address, if necessary.

4. Click the Omit check box if you don't want your return
address to appear on the envelope.

5. Click the Print button.

Two commands on the Envelopes tab tell Word how your printer
handles envelopes and what size your envelopes are.

Click the envelope icon below the word "Feed" to choose the right
technique for feeding envelopes to your printer. Click one of the
Feed Method boxes, click the Face Up or Face Down option button,
and pull down the Feed From menu to tell Word which printer tray
the envelope is in or how you intend to stick the envelope in your
printer. Click OK when you're done.

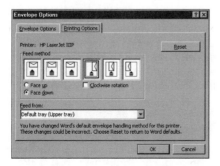

After you've fed the envelope to your printer, click the envelope icon below the word "Preview" — that's right, click the icon — to tell Word what size your envelopes are and choose other settings:

✦ **Envelope Size:** Pull down the menu and select the right size.

✦ **Delivery Point Bar Code:** Click here to put bar codes on the envelope and help the United States Postal Service deliver the letter faster.

✦ **FIM-A Courtesy Reply Mail:** Click here to put Facing Identification Marks on the envelope. These marks, which tell letter-processing machines at the post office whether the envelope is face up, also aid the speedy delivery of mail.

✦ **Delivery Address:** Change the font of the delivery address and the address's position. Change the From Left and From Top settings to slide the address up or down on the envelope.

✦ **Return Address:** Ditto for the return address.

FIM marks

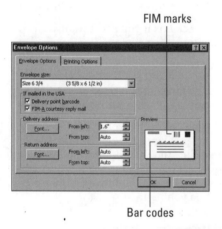

Bar codes

That Add to Document button on the Envelopes tab of the Envelopes and Labels dialog box creates a new section at the top of the document with the return and delivery address in it. In the new section, both addresses are formatted and made ready to go straight to the printer. Not everyone can take advantage of this feature. Click the Add to Document button only if you have a printer that can accept envelopes as easily as it can accept sheets of paper. (I want one for my birthday.)

To make your name and return address appear automatically in the Return Address box, choose Tools⇨Options, click the User Information tab, and enter your name and address in the Mailing Address box.

Printing on Different-Sized Paper

You don't have to print exclusively on standard 8.5 x 11 paper; you can print on legal-size paper and other sizes of paper as well. A 'zine or newsletter with an unusual shape really stands out in a crowd and gets people's attention.

To change the size of the paper on which you intend to print a document:

1. Choose File⇔Page Setup.

2. Click the Paper Size tab.

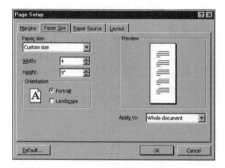

3. Choose a setting from the Paper Size drop-down list. If none of the settings suits you, enter your own settings in the Width and Height text boxes.

4. Choose an Apply To option:

   • **Whole document** for the entire document.

   • **This section** if your document has more than one section.

   • **This point forward** to create a new section and change the paper size for the rest of the document.

5. Click OK.

If you keep legal-size paper in one tray of your printer and standard-size paper in another, for example, click the Paper Source tab in the Page Setup dialog box and change settings there. ***See also*** "Landscape Documents" in Part VI to learn how to print landscape, not portrait, documents.

Click the Default button in the Paper Size tab of the Page Setup dialog box if you want your choice of paper size to be the default — the choice that is made whenever you open a new document.

Printing a Document

The fastest way to print a document is to click the Print button on the Standard toolbar. Go this route if you want to print the entire thing from start to finish. (Before you print a document, however, you ought to "preview" it by pressing the Print Preview button or by choosing File➪Print Preview.)

To print part of a document, selected text in a document, the entire thing, or even unusual things like comments and summary text, follow these steps:

1. Choose File➪Print (or press Ctrl+P) to open the Print dialog box.

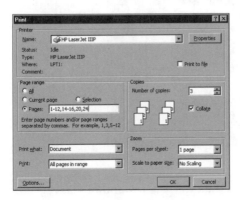

2. Enter the number of copies you want in the Number of Copies box.

3. Choose a Page Range option to tell Word how much of the document to print:

* **All:** Prints the whole thing.

* **Current Page:** Prints the page where the cursor is. Choose this option when you find an error on a page and you need to reprint it.

* **Selection:** Prints the text that was selected.

* **Pages:** Prints certain pages only. Enter hyphens to designate the page range and commas, too, if you want to print more than one page range. For example, entering **1-4** prints pages 1, 2, 3, and 4; but entering **1,4** prints pages 1 and 4 only.

4. Choose Print to File to copy the document to a print file. You might do this in order to take your document to a print shop and have it printed there. If you choose this option and click OK, the Print to File dialog box appears. Choose a name for the print file and click OK.

5. Click OK.

The Print dialog box also offers these options:

✦ **Collate:** If you're printing more than one copy of a document with many pages and you don't want the copies to be collated, click the Collate box to remove the check mark. If you print three three-page documents, for example, the pages will come out of the printer 111, 222, 333, instead of 123, 123, 123.

✦ **Print What:** Choose one of the admittedly strange options on the Print What drop-down list to print the comments in your document, AutoText entries, examples of the styles you've used, key assignments you've used, or the document property information.

✦ **Print:** Choose Odd Pages or Even Pages from the Print menu to print those pages only. This is the option to choose if you want to print on both sides of the paper. Print the odd pages, turn the pages over and feed them to your printer, and then print the even pages.

✦ **Zoom:** These options are for printing pages in miniature to see how a desktop-published document or set of Web pages are shaping up. From the Pages Per Sheet drop-down list, choose how many miniature pages to print on each sheet of paper. The more you print, the smaller the pages are. In the Scale to Paper Size drop-down list, choose the size of paper you are printing on.

Printing sections in a document can be very problematic, especially if the pages in each section are numbered differently. To print an entire section, enter an **s** and then the section number in the Print dialog box's Pages box. For example, to print Section 6, enter **s6**. To print pages within a section, enter a **p** and then the page number. For example, to print pages 4 through 10 in Section 6, enter **p4s6-p10s6**.

Printing Labels

You can print pages of labels in Word, and single labels, too. Needless to say, printing labels makes mass mailing and bulk mailing much easier. Before you start printing labels, however, note what size and what brand your labels are. You are asked about label sizes when you print labels.

Printing labels one at a time

To print mailing labels, follow these steps:

1. Open the document that contains the address of the label you want to print, and select the address.

2. Choose Tools⇨Envelopes and Labels.

3. Click the Labels tab. The address appears in the Address box. If the name or address is wrong, now's the time to fix it. If you're printing labels with your return address on them, click the Use Return Address box or enter your return address.

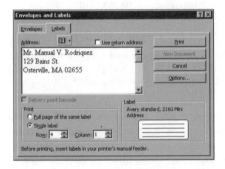

4. Either click the Options button or click the label icon in the Label box. The Label Options dialog box appears.

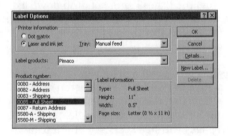

5. In the Printer Information area, click either Dot Matrix or Laser and Ink Jet to say which kind of printer you have. Then pull down the Tray drop-down list and click the option that describes how you will feed the labels to your printer.

6. Click the Label Products drop-down list and choose the brand or type of labels that you have.

   If your brand is not on the list, you can choose Other (found at the bottom of the list), click the Details button, and describe your labels in the extremely confusing Address Information dialog box. A better way, however, is to measure your labels and see whether you can find a label of the same size by experimenting with Label Products option and Product Number combinations.

7. In the Product Number box, click the product number listed on the box your labels came in. Look in the Label Information box on the right to make sure that the Height, Width, and Page Size measurements match those of the labels you have.

8. Click OK to go back to the Envelopes and Labels dialog box.

9. Choose a Print option:

- **Full Page of the Same Label:** Click this box if you want to print a pageful of the same label. Likely, you'd choose this option to print a pageful of your own return addresses. Click the New Document button after you make this choice. Word creates a new document with a pageful of labels. Save and print this document.

- **Single Label:** Click this box to print one label. Then enter the row and column where the label is and click the Print button.

Printing labels for mass mailings

To print a mess of labels for mass or bulk mailings, Word offers the Mail Merge Helper. The best way to use this nifty tool is to create a table (or a database table if you are adept with Access 2000 or another database program) with the label addressees. *See also:* "Constructing the Perfect Table" in Part III to find out how to create tables. After you have created the addresses table, save it as a file and make sure that nothing is in the file except the table itself. You can use your addresses table over and over again for printing labels and for form letters as well.

To use the Mail Merge Helper to create a file of address labels:

1. Open a new document and choose Tools⇨Mail Merge. The Mail Merge Helper opens.

2. Click the Create button and then click Mailing Labels in the drop-down list.

3. In the message box, click Active Window to add the labels to the new document that you just opened.

4. Under Step 2 in the Mail Merge Helper, click Get Data to see the menu of choices for getting the mailing label addresses, and choose Open Data Source from the menu. With this option, you get the names and addresses from a mailing list table that you or somebody else has already created and saved in a file.

5. In the Open Data Source dialog box, find the document that holds the table with your addresses, select it, and click the Open button.

6. In the message box that appears, click the Set Up Main Document button.

7. Choose options in the Label Options dialog box. This is where you tell Word what size the labels are. If these options are new to you, consult Steps 5 through 7 in the preceding section of this book, "Printing labels one at a time." Click OK when you're done. The Create Labels dialog box appears.

8. In this dialog box, you create the sample label that Word will use as a model for all the labels on the list. To do that, place the cursor in the Sample Label box where you want the addressee's name to go, click Insert Merge Field, and choose the name from the top of the drop-down list. It appears in the Sample Label box.

9. Press Enter to go to the next line in the Sample Label box, click Insert Merge Field again, and enter the next line in the address, probably the street number and street name. Press Enter again.

10. Insert the city name, state, and zip code. Enter a comma and a space after the city name, and another space after the state.

Whatever you do, don't erase the angle brackets (<<>>) or press Enter inside them. The brackets are there to mark off the parts of the address.

11. You can enter a postal bar code with the Insert Postal Bar Code button and drop-down list. In the Insert Postal Bar Code dialog box, choose the sample zip code from the drop-down list.

12. Click OK.

13. Back in the Mail Merge Helper, click the Merge button. You see the Merge dialog box.

14. Make sure that the <u>D</u>on't Print Blank Lines When Data Fields Are Empty box is checked. This prevents blank lines from appearing in your labels.

15. Click the <u>M</u>erge button. Word generates the mailing labels in a file called Labels1, and you get something like this:

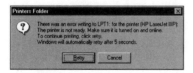

  If you want, you can choose a new font for the labels by pressing Ctrl+A to select the document and then choosing a new font from the Font drop-down list.

16. Choose <u>F</u>ile⇨<u>S</u>ave, press Ctrl+S, or click the Save button and save your label file under a new name in the Save As dialog box.

17. Now that your labels are on disk, put a blank sheet of labels in the printer and print your new labels.

Solving Problems with the Printer

Occasionally, you try to print a document and get this disconcerting message or one like it:

In David Letterman fashion, here is a top-ten list of things to do when you can't print a document or a document doesn't print correctly:

10. Is text running off the page? You may have attempted to print on paper that is the wrong size. Choose <u>F</u>ile⇨Page Set<u>u</u>p, click the Paper <u>S</u>ize tab, and change the Pape<u>r</u> Size options.

9. Are your graphics not printing? Choose <u>T</u>ools⇨<u>O</u>ptions, click the Print tab, and click the <u>D</u>raft Output check box to remove the check mark.

8. You keep getting the same printer error message? You may have selected the wrong printer. Choose File⇨Print and choose another printer from the Name drop-down list. If that doesn't work, try reinstalling your printer with the Add New Hardware application in the Windows Control Panel.

7. The gridlines don't appear in tables? That's because you haven't given your table borders or you're printing on a dot-matrix printer, which doesn't print table lines very well.

6. You've loaded envelopes in the printer, but Word still doesn't budge? Probably you put the envelopes in the wrong tray. Choose Tools⇨Envelopes and Labels, click the Envelopes tab, click the envelope inside the Feed box, and choose the correct method of loading envelopes in your printer.

5. Do fonts look different on-screen than they do on paper? Your printer may not be able to handle certain fonts, in which case you have to find substitutes among the TrueType fonts you have. TrueType fonts look the same on-screen as they do when printed. You can tell a TrueType font on the Font menu because it has a *TT* next to its name.

4. Are lines breaking in strange places? Your margins may be too wide. Change the margin settings.

3. You keep seeing the `There is an error writing to your printer` message? You may have sent too many print jobs to the printer. Wait for your printer to digest what you've already sent it and try again.

2. Does Word tell you `There was an error writing to` blah blah blah? You may be out of paper. Or maybe the printer cables aren't hooked up correctly.

1. Are you getting nothing but error messages? See whether the printer is turned on. If it's not on, you can't print.

Making Your Work Go Faster

Computers are supposed to make your work easier and faster. And if you can cut through all the jargon and technobabble, they can really do that.

Part V explains shortcuts and commands that can help you become a speedy user of Word 2000. Everything in this part of the book is put here so that you can get off work an hour earlier and take the slow, scenic route home.

In this part . . .

- ✔ Moving around quickly in long documents
- ✔ Creating form letters by merging letters with names and addresses in a database table
- ✔ Linking files
- ✔ Entering data quickly with forms
- ✔ Using outlines to organize your work
- ✔ Customizing Word so that it works for you

Bookmarks for Hopping Around

Instead of pressing PgUp or PgDn or clicking the scrollbar to thrash around in a long document, you can use bookmarks. All you do is put a bookmark in an important spot in your document that you'll return to many times. When you want to return to that spot, choose Insert⇨Bookmark, double-click the bookmark in the Bookmark dialog box, and click Cancel.

This mystery writer, true to the craft, wrote the end of the story first and used bookmarks to jump back and forth between the beginning and end to make all the clues fit together:

To place a bookmark in a document:

1. Click where you want the bookmark to go.

2. Choose Insert⇨Bookmark (or press Ctrl+Shift+F5).

3. Type a descriptive name in the Bookmark Name box. You cannot include spaces in bookmark names.

4. Click the Add button.

To go to a bookmark:

1. Choose Insert⇨Bookmark (or press Ctrl+Shift+F5).

2. Double-click the bookmark or select it and click the Go To button.

3. Click Cancel or press Esc.

You can arrange bookmarks in the list in alphabetical order or by location in the document by choosing Name or Location at the bottom of the Bookmark dialog box. Click the Hidden bookmarks check box to see cross-references in the Bookmark Name box, although hidden bookmarks appear as code and don't tell you much about what they are or where they are in the document.

To delete a bookmark, select it in the Bookmark dialog box and click the Delete button.

Churning Out Form Letters

Thanks to the miracle of computing, you can churn out form letters in the privacy of your home or office, just like the big companies do. To create form letters, you complete three steps:

1. Create the *main document,* the document with the actual text of the letter.

2. Create the *source document,* the document with the names, addresses, and any other text that differs from letter to letter.

You can create the source document as you merge documents, but that is a waste of time. A better way is to create a Word table as the source document. That way, you can reuse the source document for mass mailings or form letters as often as you want. ***See also*** "Constructing the Perfect Table" in Part III to find out how to create a table in Word. Make sure that nothing is in the source document except the table and that the table has a header row along the top that labels the information below it. For example, a table of names and addresses would have a header row with these labels: Name, Street, City, State, and Zip.

3. Merge the two documents to generate the form letters.

Before you generate the form letter, write a first draft. That way, you will know precisely what information varies from recipient to recipient — the names and addresses, for example — before you start generating the letter. Your Word table must contain all the variable information that you will add to the main document when you merge the documents and generate the form letters.

This figure shows the first draft of the letter (the main document) and the table with information for the form letter (the source document). Variable information is in boldface:

Name
Street
City, State Zip

Dear **Name**,

It was a pleasure serving you last **season**. May your
holidays be joyful and loving.

Sincerely,
The Lighthouse Staff

Name	Street	City	State	Zip	Season
Mr. Clyde T. Haines	1289 Durham Lane	Osterville	MA	02655	Summer
Ms. Gladys Yee	1293 Durham Lane	Osterville	MA	02655	Summer
Ms. Esther Harmony	2601 Estner Rd.	Osterville	MA	02655	Fall
Ms. Melinda Sings	2789 Estner Rd.	Osterville	MA	02655	Spring
Mr. Rupert S. Stickenmud	119 Scutter Lane	Osterville	MA	02655	Fall
Ms. Martha Hines	1263 Tick Park	Osterville	MA	02655	Summer

Follow these steps to generate form letters:

1. Open the main document, the one with the text of the letter, if
it is not already open.

2. Choose Tools➪Mail Merge. The Mail Merge Helper dialog box
appears.

3. Click the Create button and choose Form Letters from the
drop-down list.

4. A message box asks if you want to create the form letters in
the active document or in a new document. Click the Active
Window button.

5. Under Step 2 in the Mail Merge Helper, click Get Data and
choose Open Data Source from the drop-down list.

6. In the Open Data Source dialog box, locate the source document with your addresses and other variable information,
select the document, and click the Open button.

7. In the message box that appears, click the Edit Main
Document button. Back in the main document, the Mail Merge
toolbar appears along the top of the screen. On the toolbar's
Insert Merge Field drop-down list are the names of each
column from the source table whose data you will put in the
form letter.

8. One by one, go to each piece of variable information in the
table, erase it if necessary, and choose a field from the Insert
Merge Field drop-down list. Field names appear in brackets in
the letter after you insert them. Make sure that the punctuation and spacing around the field names are correct. For
example, a comma should go after "Dear <<Name>>".

When you are done, your form letter looks something like this (without the table, of course — it only appears in the figure so that you can see how information from the source document lands on the Insert Merge Field menu):

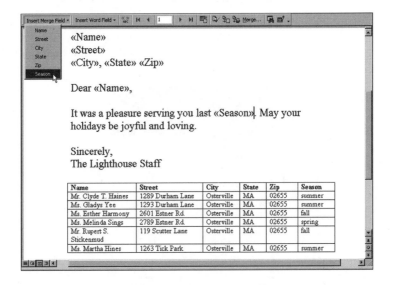

9. Click the <u>M</u>erge button on the Mail Merge toolbar to start merging the main document and source document. You see the Merge dialog box.

10. Make a choice on the Me<u>r</u>ge To drop-down list and then click the <u>M</u>erge button to merge the fill-in-the-blanks in the main document with the information from the source document:

- **New Document:** Creates a new document with all the form letters in it. A document like this can be very long if the source document includes many records (rows with information in them). After you click the <u>M</u>erge button, your new document appears on-screen. Save it and then print the form letters.

• **Printer:** Prints the form letters without saving them in a document. This option saves disk space because the merged letters are not saved on disk. After you click the <u>M</u>erge button, you see the Print dialog box. Make sure that your printer is on and click OK to print the form letters.

This figure shows a form letter after the main document and source document were merged. Notice how smoothly the information in the first row of the source table fits into the form letter.

Mr. Clyde T. Haines
1289 Durham Lane
Osterville, MA 02655

Dear Mr. Clyde T. Haines,

It was a pleasure serving you last summer. May your holidays be joyful and loving.

Sincerely,
The Lighthouse Staff

Correcting Typos on the Fly

Unless you or someone else has messed with the AutoCorrect settings, the invisible hand of Word corrects certain typos as you enter them. Try misspelling *weird* by typing *wierd* to see what I mean. Try entering two hyphens (--) and you get an em dash (—). You can have Word correct the typos that you make often, and with a little cunning, you can even use the AutoCorrect feature to enter long company names and hard-to-spell names on the fly.

To change the settings and make AutoCorrect work for you, choose <u>T</u>ools⇨<u>A</u>utoCorrect. The AutoCorrect dialog box appears.

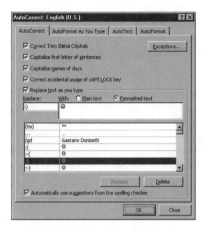

✦ Remove the check marks from the AutoCorrect features that you don't want. For example, if you enter a lot of computer code in your manuscripts, you don't necessarily want the first letter of sentences to be capitalized automatically, so you should click the Capitalize First Letter of Sentences check box to deselect it.

✦ If you want, remove the check mark from the Replace Text as You Type box to keep Word's invisible hand from correcting idiosyncrasies in capitalization and spelling as you enter them.

✦ Scroll through the list and take a look at the words that are "autocorrected." If you don't want a word on the list to be corrected, select it and click Delete.

✦ If a word that you often misspell isn't on the list, you can add it to the list and have Word correct it automatically. Enter the misspelling in the Replace box, enter the right spelling in the With box, and click the Add button.

✦ If you don't like one of the replacement words, select the word on the list, enter a new replacement word in the With box, and click the Replace button.

The Spelling dialog box has an AutoCorrect option. Choose it when you're spell-checking a document to add the word you're correcting to the list of words that are "autocorrected." The AutoCorrect choice also appears on the shortcut menu when you right-click a misspelled word. Choose AutoCorrect on the shortcut menu and choose a correct spelling to add the misspelling to the family of words that get corrected automatically.

Customizing Word 2000

You can make Word 2000 work your way by putting the menu commands in different places, inventing your own keyboard shortcuts for executing commands, and even creating your own toolbars. *See also* "Rearranging the Toolbars," also in Part V, to discover how to make toolbars with your favorite command buttons on them. Read on to find out how to change the menu commands and designate your own keyboard shortcuts. Believe me, changing the menus around is well worth your while if you are a speed demon who likes to get work done fast.

Changing the menu commands

You can decide for yourself which menu commands appear on which menus. You can also add macros, fonts, AutoText entries, and styles to menus. Doing so is easy, and if you make a mistake and want to go back to the original menus, that is easy, too.

The quickest (but scariest) way to remove a command from a menu is to press Ctrl+Alt+hyphen. When the cursor changes into an ominous black bar, simply select the menu command that you want to remove. Press Esc, by the way, if you decide after you press Ctrl+Alt+hyphen that you don't want to remove menu commands. (See the tip at the end of this section if you removed menu commands this way and now you want them back.)

A more precise way to remove menu commands or alter the menus is to use the Commands tab of the Customize dialog box:

1. Choose Tools⇨Customize.

2. Click the Commands tab.

3. If you want the menu changes you make to be made to a template other than Normal.dot or the template you are working in, choose the template in the Save In drop-down list.

4. In the Categories list, select the menu you want to change. If you're adding a macro, font, AutoText entry, or style to a menu, scroll to the bottom of the Categories list and select it. The commands that are on the menu you chose appear in the Commands list on the right.

5. Choose the command you're changing in the Commands list. You can click the Description button to read a description of the command if you aren't quite sure what it does.

6. What you do next depends on whether you want to remove a command from a menu, add a command to a menu, or change its position on a menu. Changing menu commands requires moving the pointer out of the Customize dialog box and clicking menus on the menu bar.

- **Removing:** To remove a menu command, move the pointer over the menu that holds the command you want to remove and click gently. That's right — click the menu name as you normally would if you were pulling it down to choose one of its commands. When the menu appears, click the menu command you want to remove, and drag it off the menu. You see a gray rectangle above the pointer and an *X* below it. Release the mouse button after you have dragged the menu command away from the menu.

- **Adding:** To add a menu command to a menu, drag it from the Commands list in the Customize dialog box to the menu itself. As you do this, you see a gray rectangle above the pointer and a plus sign below it. Move the pointer over the menu to which you want to add the command. The menu appears. Gently drag the pointer down the menu to the spot where you want the command to be listed. A black line appears on the menu to show where your command will go. When the command is in the right spot, release the mouse button.

- **Changing position:** To change the position of a command on a menu, move the pointer out of the Customize dialog box and gently click on the menu whose command you want to move. Then drag the pointer up or down the list of commands. A black line shows where the command will move when you release the mouse button. When the black line is in the right spot, let up on the mouse button.

7. Click Close.

If you wish that you hadn't messed with the menus and want to repent, choose Tools⇨Customize, click the Commands tab, move the pointer out of the dialog box, right-click the name of the menu whose commands you fooled with, and choose Reset from the shortcut menu.

Changing the keyboard shortcuts

If you don't like Word's keyboard shortcuts, you can change them and invent keyboard shortcuts of your own. You can also assign keyboard shortcuts to symbols, macros, fonts, AutoText entries, and styles.

1. Choose Tools⇨Customize.

2. Click the Keyboard button. You see the Customize Keyboard dialog box.

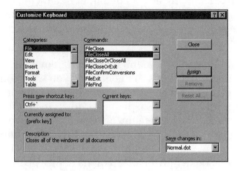

3. To make the changes to a template other than Normal.dot or the template you are working in, choose a template in the . Save Changes In drop-down list.

4. In the Categories list, choose the menu with the command to which you want to assign the keyboard shortcut. At the bottom of the list are the Macro, Font, AutoText, Style, and Common Symbols categories.

5. Choose the command name, macro, font, AutoText entry, style, or symbol name in the Commands list.

6. Click in the Press New Shortcut Key box and type the keyboard shortcut. Press the actual keys. For example, if the shortcut is Ctrl+~, press the Ctrl key and the ~ key — don't type out C-t-r-l-+~.

If you try to assign a shortcut that is already assigned, the words Currently assigned to and a command name appear below the Press New Shortcut Key box. You can override the preassigned keyboard assignment by entering a keyboard assignment of your own.

7. Click the Assign button.

8. When you're done, click the Close button.

9. Click Close in the Customize dialog box.

To delete a keyboard shortcut, display it in the Current Keys box, click it to select it, and click the Remove button.

You can always get the old keyboard shortcuts back by choosing the Reset All button in the Customize Keyboard dialog box. Click Yes when Word asks whether you really want the old keyboard shortcuts back.

Entering Graphics and Text Quickly

Put the text and graphics that you often use on the Insert⇨ AutoText list. That way, you can enter the text or graphics simply by clicking a few menu commands or by choosing names from a toolbar. Addresses, letterheads, and company logos are ideal candidates for the AutoText list because they take so long to enter.

Creating your own AutoText entries

Follow these steps to create an AutoText entry:

1. Type the text or import the graphic.

2. Select the text or graphic.

3. Choose Insert⇨AutoText⇨New or press Alt+F3. The Create AutoText dialog box appears:

4. Type a name for the text or graphic in the text box and click OK.

You can also create a text entry by choosing Insert⇨AutoText⇨ AutoText. In the AutoCorrect dialog box, click the AutoText tab, and then type the word or phrase in the Enter AutoText Entries Here box. Click Add and then OK when you're done.

Inserting an AutoText entry

The fastest way to insert an AutoText entry is to place the cursor where you want it to go and start typing the entry's name. Midway through, a bubble appears with the entire entry. Press Enter at that point to insert the whole thing:

Another speedy way to insert AutoText entries is to type the entry's name and then press F3.

AutoText entries that you create yourself appear on the Normal submenu. Follow these steps to insert one of your own AutoText entries or one that comes with Word:

1. Place the cursor where you want the text or graphic to appear.

2. Choose Insert⇨AutoText⇨Normal and select an entry, or choose an entry from one of the submenus below Normal.

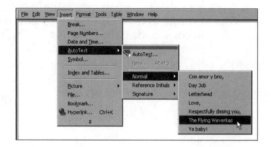

Not to belabor the point, but yet another way to insert an AutoText entry is to display the AutoText toolbar, click the drop-down list, choose Normal or another submenu, and click an entry.

To delete an AutoText entry, choose Insert⇨AutoText⇨AutoText to open the AutoCorrect dialog box, click the AutoText tab, click the entry that you want to delete, and click the Delete button.

Those yellow AutoText bubbles can be very annoying. They pop up in the oddest places. Try typing the name of a month, for example, to see what I mean. To keep the bubbles from appearing, choose Insert⇨AutoText⇨AutoText and click to remove the check mark from the Show AutoComplete Tip for AutoText and Dates check box.

Entering Information Quickly with Forms

A *form* is a means of soliciting and recording information. Besides creating paper forms, you can create computerized forms that make entering data easy. Designing computerized forms is a tricky business and is too complicated for this little book, but this section will at least get you started.

Creating a paper form

To create paper forms, use commands on the Table menu. By shading cells, by merging cells, by drawing borders around different parts of the table, and by using different fonts, you can create a form like the one shown here. (*See also* "Constructing the Perfect Table" in Part III to find out how to work with tables.) In this figure, the table is shown first with only the text and the gridlines. Borders and shading have been added to different parts of the final, completed table to make it look like a form.

Name				For Official Use Only
	Last	First	Middle	
Address				Arrival:
	Number and Street			
	City	State	Zip	Departure:
Phones	( )			
	( )	Please list numbers where you can be reached 9:00 A.M. to 5 P.M.		TLC: Yes ☐ No ☐

Name				For Official Use Only
	Last	First	Middle	
Address				Arrival:
	Number and Street			
	City	State	Zip	Departure:
Phones	( )			
	( )	Please list numbers where you can be reached 9:00 A.M. to 5 P.M.		TLC: Yes ☐ No ☐

Creating a computerized form

A computerized form is an electronic version of a paper form. Computerized forms make entering data easier because the person who enters the data can type only in predefined areas — the person can't erase the names of the fields where data is entered. If you were to turn the paper form in the previous figure into a computerized form, you or someone else could then enter the data from the paper forms into a computer file very quickly and cleanly.

The first step to creating a computerized form is to design the form. Enter the names of the fields — the places where information goes — and leave empty spaces for the information itself. Instead of designing the computerized form from scratch, you can use a paper form that you created with Microsoft Word.

After you have designed the form, you turn it into a template and tell Word where the fields are. With that done, you choose File⇨New, choose the template that you created for your new file, and open the file. Then you enter the raw data itself. You can enter data in the predefined fields only. When you are done, you have a file with all the data in it.

Here is how to create a computerized form:

1. Open a new document or, if you have already designed a paper form and want to turn it into an electronic form, open the paper form. Label the fields appropriately and make sure that enough room is on the form to enter the raw data you will enter later.

2. Choose File⇨Save As. You are going to save the document as a template.

3. Click the down arrow to open the Save As Type menu and choose Document Template (*.dot). The template folder's name appears in the Save In box.

4. Type a name for the template in the File Name box.

5. Click the Save button.

Now that the form is a template, you have to put input fields in it so that you can enter the raw data. A *field* is simply a piece of information. Input fields fall into three categories:

✦ **Text:** A text entry, such as a name, address, or telephone number.

✦ **Check box:** A "multiple choice," such as two or three check boxes, only one of which can be selected.

✦ **Drop-down:** A drop-down list of choices.

To enter input field types, open the Forms toolbar. Do that by right-clicking on a toolbar and choosing Forms from the shortcut menu. To enter the input fields:

1. Go to the first place in the template where data is to be entered.

2. Click the Text Form Field, Check Box Form Field, or Drop-Down Form Field button on the Forms toolbar, depending on the type of field you need. When you do so, Word puts shading on the form where the field is. (If you don't see the shading, click the Form Field Shading button on the Forms toolbar.)

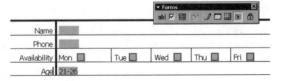

3. Keep going down the template and entering form fields. In this form, I have entered eight fields. The five in the second-to-last row are Check Box Form Fields, and the last field is a Drop-Down Form Field.

Don't worry about the fields' length. Unless you click the Form Field Options button and change the settings, text of any length can be entered in input fields. However, you may want to change the length setting in a zip code field to keep anyone from inputting more than nine numbers, for example.

4. When you're done entering the input fields, click the Protect Form button. Now whoever enters the data on the form cannot disturb the field names. He or she can type in only the input fields.

5. Save the template and close it.

Now that you have the template, you can enter data cleanly in easy-to-read forms:

1. Choose File⇔New to open a new document to enter the data in. The template that you created appears on the General tab of the New dialog box.

2. Double-click the template you created.

3. Enter information in the input fields. Press the up or down arrow, or press Tab and Shift+Tab to move from field to field. You can also click input fields to move the cursor there. Notice that you can't change the field labels.

4. When you're done, either print the document or save it.

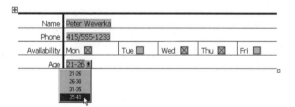

Going Here, Going There in Documents

Word offers three very speedy techniques for jumping around in documents: the Select Browse Object button, the Edit⇔Go To command, and the document map.

"Browsing" around a document

A really fast way to move around quickly is to click the Select Browse Object button in the lower-right corner of the screen. When you click this button, Word presents the "Browse by" icons:

Select the icon that represents the element you want to go to, and Word takes you there immediately. For example, click the Browse by Heading icon to get to the next heading in your document (provided that you assigned a heading style to the heading). After you have selected a "Browse by" icon, the navigator buttons — the double-arrows directly above and below the Select Browse Object button — turn blue. Click a blue navigator button to get to the next example or the previous example of the element you chose. For example, if you selected the Browse by Heading icon, all you have to do is click blue navigator buttons to get from heading to heading backwards or forwards in a document.

Going there fast

Another fast way to go from place to place in a document is to use the Edit⇨Go To command. Choose this command or press Ctrl+G to see the Go To tab of the Find and Replace dialog box:

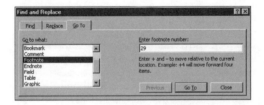

The Go to What menu in this dialog box lists everything that can conceivably be numbered in a Word document, and other things, too. Everything that you can get to with the Select Browse Object button, as well as lines, equations, and objects, can be reached by way of the Go To tab. Click a menu item and enter a number or choose an item from the drop-down list to go elsewhere.

Click the Previous button to go back to the footnote, endnote, comment, line, or whatever you just came from. You can press + or – and enter numbers to go backward or forward by one or several numbered items at once.

Hopping from place to place

Yet another way to hop from place to place is by turning on the document map. To do so, click the Document Map button or choose View⇨Document Map. Everything in the document that hasn't been assigned the Normal style — headings, captions, and so on — appears along the left side of the screen.

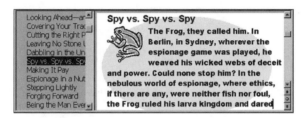

By placing the pointer on the text that doesn't fit on-screen, you can read it. Click the heading, caption, or whatever you want to go to, and Word takes you there in the twinkling of an eye. Right-click the document map and choose a heading level option from the shortcut menu to tell Word which headings to display in the map. To put away the document map and see only the document on-screen, click the Document Map button again.

Linking Documents to Make Your Work Easier

You can save a lot of time and effort by connecting two documents so that changes made to the first are made automatically to the second. This process is called *linking*. If a table in a memo you are working on happens to be useful in an annual report as well, you can link the documents, and updates to the table in the memo will show up in the annual report as well.

Word offers two kinds of links, automatic and manual:

✦ With an *automatic link,* changes made to the original document are made in the linked document as well each time you reopen the linked document. Text is displayed in full in your document if the link is automatic.

✦ With a *manual link,* you have to tell Word to update the link. Manual links are represented in the text by an icon. The text or graphic in the original file does not appear in your document.

Creating a link

Before you create a link between documents, ask yourself whether either document is likely to be moved out of the folder where it is now. Links are broken when documents are moved. Although you can reestablish a link, doing so is a chore. The better strategy is to plan ahead and link only documents that are not going to be moved to different folders. Follow these steps to create an automatic link between documents:

1. Open the document with the text you want to link.

2. Select the text and copy it to the Clipboard by clicking the Copy button, pressing Ctrl+C, or choosing Edit⇔Copy.

3. Switch to the document where the linked text is to be pasted and put the cursor where you want the text to go.

4. Choose Edit⇔Paste Special. The Paste Special dialog box appears.

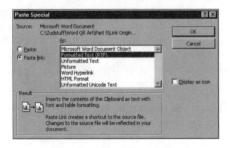

5. Click the Paste Link radio button.

6. Under As, choose Formatted Text (RTF) or Unformatted Text; otherwise, if the thing being linked is not text, choose another option.

7. Click OK.

Updating, breaking, and changing links

With an automatic link, changes made to the original document are made to the linked document whenever the linked document is reopened. With manual links, however, you have to tell Word to update the link.

To update a link — and do other things besides — go to the Links dialog box:

1. Choose Edit⇔Links.

2. In the Links dialog box, select the link you want to update. Be sure to look at the Source File listing at the bottom of the dialog box to make sure that you're updating the right link.

3. Click the Update Now button.

4. Click OK.

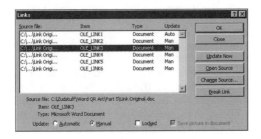

You can update several links at the same time by Ctrl+clicking the links before you click the Update Now button.

The Links dialog box offers several more buttons and check boxes for handling links:

✦ **Open Source:** Opens the original document so that you can make changes to text.

✦ **Change Source:** If you move the original document to another folder, Word doesn't know where to look for the document that contains the original text. Click this button to open the Change Source dialog box. Then find the original document and click Open. The link is reestablished.

✦ **Break Link:** Severs the tie between the original document and the document with the link in it. Once you click this button, the link is broken, and you can't get it back.

✦ **Automatic:** Click this option button to change the link to an automatic link.

✦ **Manual:** Click to change the link to a manual link.

✦ **Locked:** Makes it so that updates to the original document do not affect the linked document. Choose this option instead of Break Link if you want to break the link but still be able to go to the original document if you have to.

✦ **Save Picture in Document:** Saves a graphic in your document instead of a link to the graphic. Uncheck this check box to store a link to the graphic.

Suppose that you're in the linked document and you realize that you need to change the original text. If the link is a manual one, all you have to do is double-click the Microsoft Word Document icon to get to the original text. With an automatic link, choose Edit⇨ Linked Document Object⇨Open Link, or right-click and choose Linked Document Object⇨Open Link from the shortcut menu.

To make sure that all links are updated before you print documents, choose Tools⇨Options, click the Print tab, and click the Update Links check box.

Besides links, you can also create *hyperlinks* — a link between two documents or between two different places in the same document or between a document and a location on the Internet. By clicking a hyperlink, you go directly to the other document or other place in the same document. **See also** "Hyperlinking your Web page to other pages" in Part VI to discover how to put a hyperlink in a document.

Outlines for Organizing Your Work

Outline view is a great way to see at a glance how your document is organized and whether you need to organize it differently. To take advantage of this feature, you must have used the Style menu to assign heading levels to the headings in your document. (**See also** "Applying Styles for Consistent Formatting" in Part III.) In Outline view, you can see all the headings in your document. If a section is in the wrong place, you can move it simply by dragging an icon or by pressing one of the buttons on the Outline toolbar.

To see a document in Outline view, choose View⇨Outline or click the Outline View button in the lower-left corner of the screen. Here is a sample document in Outline view with the All button selected to show all the headings and the normal text in paragraphs.

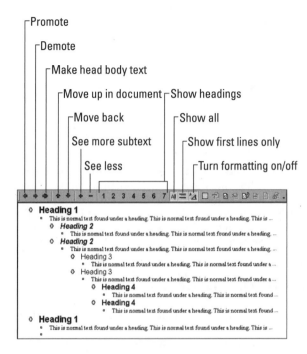

Promote

Demote

Make head body text

Move up in document — Show headings

Move back — Show all

See more subtext — Show first lines only

See less — Turn formatting on/off

To change how much of a document you see in Outline view:

✦ **Headings:** Click a Show Heading button (1 through 7) to see different heading levels.

✦ **All:** Click the All button to see the whole show.

✦ **Headings in one section:** If you want to see the headings and text in only one section of a document, choose that section by clicking the plus sign beside it and then click the Expand button. Click the Collapse button when you're done.

✦ **Normal text:** Click the Show First Line Only button to see only the first line in each paragraph. First lines are followed by an ellipsis (. . .) so that you know that more text follows.

Notice the plus icons and square icons next to the headings and the text. A plus icon means that the heading has subtext under it. For example, headings almost always have plus icons because text comes after them, but body text has a square icon because it is lowest on the Outline totem pole.

To select text in Outline view, click either the plus sign or the square icon. To select more than one section, Shift+click its icon. After the text has been selected, you can do the following tasks:

✦ **Promote a head:** Click the Promote button to move a heading up the ladder. For example, you can promote a Heading 2 to a Heading 1.

✦ **Demote a head:** Click the Demote button to bust down a Heading 1 to a Heading 2, for example. When you promote or demote a head or section, you do the same to all the subtext beneath it.

✦ **Make a head into normal text:** Click the Demote to Body Text button to make a heading into text.

✦ **Move a section:** To move a section up or down in the document, click the Move Up or Move Down button. You can also drag the plus sign or square icon to a new location. If you want to move the subordinate text and headings along with the section, click the Collapse button to tuck all the subtext into the heading before you move it.

Rearranging the Toolbars

To make working with toolbars easier, you can drag them around on-screen. You can remove buttons from toolbars and replace them with buttons of your own choosing. You can even create your own toolbars and invent new toolbar buttons.

To find out what a button on a toolbar does, choose Help➪ What's This? (or press Shift+F1) and click a toolbar button. A description of the button appears on-screen. You can also move the mouse pointer over a button to read a one- or two-word description. If you're not seeing the descriptions, choose Tools➪Customize, click the Options tab of the Customize dialog box, and click the Show ScreenTips on Toolbars check box.

Displaying other toolbars

Two toolbars appear at the top of the Word window: the Standard toolbar and the Formatting toolbar. To place new toolbars in the window, right-click a toolbar and click the toolbar's name on the shortcut menu. You can also choose View➪Toolbars and click a name on the submenu. What's more, you can display the Drawing toolbar or Tables and Borders toolbar by clicking their buttons on the Standard toolbar.

After a toolbar is on-screen, try dragging it into the window and
repositioning it or changing its shape:

✦ To unanchor a toolbar that is stuck to the top or bottom of the
Word window, move the mouse pointer over the slider on the
left side of the toolbar and, when you see the four-headed
arrow, click and drag the toolbar onto the screen.

✦ To move a toolbar on-screen, drag its title bar.

✦ To change a toolbar's shape, place the mouse on a border.
When you see the two-headed arrow, drag the border until the
toolbar is the shape you want.

This figure shows all the Word toolbars on the shortcut menu.
They have been dragged into the window and reshaped.

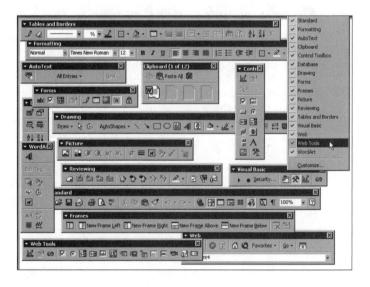

To remove a toolbar that you've dragged into the window, click its
Close button (the *X* in the upper-right corner), or choose
View➪Toolbars and click its name on the submenu. Double-click
its title bar to move it back to its rightful place at the top or
bottom of the window.

Occasionally when you click a down arrow and open a drop-down
list, you see a line along the top of the list. When you see that line,
you can turn the list into a *floating toolbar,* a menu that you can
move around on-screen like the Font Color floating toolbar shown
here. To do so, click and drag the line. You can drag a floating

toolbar anywhere you want on-screen. Floating toolbars are convenient when you want to try out different commands. Instead of having to open a menu and choose a command, you simply click different buttons on the floating toolbar until you discover the right choice.

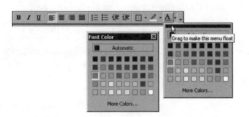

Choosing which buttons appear on toolbars

For all I know, you never do some of the tasks that the buttons on the Standard and Formatting toolbars were put there to help you do. If you're not using a button, you can take it off the toolbar and replace it with a button that you do use. Adding buttons to and removing buttons from toolbars are easy, and if you make a mistake, getting the original toolbars back is easy, too. If you don't have Microsoft Excel, for example, you can chuck the Insert Microsoft Excel Worksheet button on the Standard toolbar and put a button that you do use in its place.

The fastest way to change the buttons on a toolbar is to click the toolbar arrow on the right side of a toolbar, but you can also go to the Customize dialog box to do a more thorough job. First, the toolbar arrow method:

1. Put the toolbar whose buttons you want to change on-screen. To do so, choose View⇨Toolbar and click the toolbar's name.

2. Click the tiny arrow on the right side of the toolbar, the one directly to the right of the rightmost button.

3. Choose Add or Remove buttons, the only choice on the drop-down list. A menu appears with the names of buttons now on the toolbar. If you are dealing with the Standard or Formatting toolbar, a handful of extra buttons appears at the bottom of the list.

Check or uncheck buttons to add or remove them

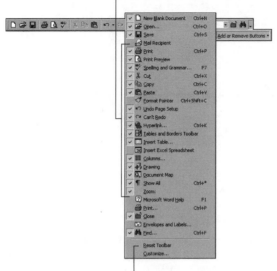

Click to get the original toolbar back

4. Click the check boxes next to button names to add or remove buttons from the toolbar. A check mark next to a button means that it appears on the toolbar.

To get the officially certified Microsoft toolbar that came with the program, click the toolbar arrow, choose Add or Remove buttons, and choose Reset Toolbar at the bottom of the buttons list.

So much for the toolbar arrow method. To do a more thorough job of customizing toolbars, to rearrange the buttons on a toolbar, or to bring buttons from distant toolbars to rest on the toolbar of your choice, follow these steps:

1. Put the toolbar that you want to customize on-screen.

2. Choose Tools⇔Customize, or right-click a toolbar and choose Customize from the shortcut menu. The Customize dialog box appears.

3. Click the Commands tab.

The Categories list in this dialog box lists all the menus and several of the toolbars. At the bottom of the list are the styles, macros, AutoText entries, and fonts that are available in the template you're using. You can find every command in Word in this dialog box by clicking an item in the Categories box and then scrolling in the Commands box. If you aren't sure what a button does, click it in the Commands box and then click the Description button.

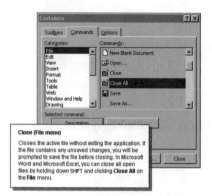

4. Remove or add a button from the toolbar you displayed in Step 1. To do so, you move the pointer outside the Customize dialog box and click toolbars at the screen:

- **Removing:** To remove a button from a toolbar, simply drag it off the toolbar. As you drag, a gray rectangle appears above the pointer, and an *X* appears below it. Release the mouse button, and the toolbar button disappears.

- **Adding:** To add a button, find it in the Customize dialog box by clicking categories and scrolling in the Commands box. When you have found the button, gently drag it out of the Customize dialog box and place it on the toolbar where you want it to appear. As you do so, a gray rectangle appears above the cursor. A plus sign appears below it when you move the button onto the toolbar.

5. While the Customize dialog box is open, you can drag buttons to new locations on toolbars.

6. If you want your new toolbar arrangement to appear only in certain templates, click the Save In drop-down list and choose the template.

7. Click Close.

You can also move buttons between toolbars by dragging them from toolbar to toolbar while the Customize dialog box is open. To copy buttons from one toolbar to another, hold down the Ctrl key as you drag the buttons.

If you make a boo-boo and wish that you hadn't fooled with the buttons on the toolbar, choose Tools⇨Customize or right-click a toolbar and choose Customize to get to the Customize dialog box. From there, click the Toolbars tab, click the toolbar whose buttons you fooled with, and click the Reset button. Click OK in the Reset Toolbar dialog box.

Creating your own toolbar

You can also create a new toolbar with your favorite buttons on it.
If you want, you can even create toolbar buttons for styles, fonts,
AutoText entries, and macros.

1. Choose Tools➪Customize, or right-click a toolbar and choose
   Customize from the shortcut menu to see the Customize
   dialog box.

2. Click the Toolbars tab.

3. Click the New button. The New Toolbar dialog box appears:

4. Type a name for your toolbar in the Toolbar Name box. The
   name you type here will appear on the View➪Toolbars
   submenu.

5. If necessary, choose a template in the Make Toolbar Available
   To drop-down list.

6. Click OK. A tiny toolbar with the name you entered appears on
   the screen.

7. Double-click the title bar of your new toolbar to move it to the
   top of the screen.

8. Click the Commands tab in the Customize dialog box.

9. In the Categories box, find and click the category in which the
   command, style, font, macro, or AutoText entry you want to
   put on a toolbar is found. You will find macros, fonts, AutoText
   entries, and styles at the bottom of the Categories menu.

10. To add a button, drag an item from the Commands box right
   onto your new toolbar. Drag as many buttons onto the toolbar
   as you need. For now, don't worry about their position on the
   toolbar. Simply drag them onto the left side, to the first
   position.

11. When you've added all the buttons, drag them where you
   want them to stand on the toolbar.

12. If you've added styles or fonts, you may want to shorten their names to make them fit better on the toolbar. To do that, right-click the button whose name you want to shorten and enter a new name in the <u>N</u>ame text box. Also on the shortcut menu are commands for changing the appearance of buttons.

13. When your toolbar is just-so, click Close.

You can always delete a toolbar you made yourself. Choose <u>T</u>ools⇨<u>C</u>ustomize, or right-click a toolbar and choose Customize to get to the Customize dialog box. Then click the Toolbars tab, click the toolbar you want to extinguish (self-made toolbars are at the bottom of the list), and click the Delete button. Click OK when Word asks if you really want to go through with it.

Repeating an Action — and Quicker This Time

The Edit menu has a command called Repeat that you can choose to repeat your last action, and it can be a mighty time-saver. The command changes names, depending on what you did last.

For example, if you just changed a heading style, the command is called <u>E</u>dit⇨<u>R</u>epeat Style. To change another heading in the same way, move the cursor to the heading and choose <u>E</u>dit⇨<u>R</u>epeat Style (or press F4 or Ctrl+Y) instead of going to the trouble of clicking the Style menu and choosing a heading style from the drop-down list.

If you had to type "I will not talk in class" a hundred times, all you would have to do is write it once and choose <u>E</u>dit⇨<u>R</u>epeat Typing (or press F4 or Ctrl+Y) 99 times.

Similar to the <u>E</u>dit⇨<u>R</u>epeat command is the Redo button. It "redoes" the commands you "undid" with the Undo menu or Undo button. If you've "undone" a bunch of commands and regret having done so, pull down the Redo menu by clicking its down arrow and choose the commands you thoughtlessly "undid" the first time around.

Web and Desktop Publishing

Once upon a time, word processors were nothing more than glorified typewriters. They were good for typing and basic formatting, but not much else. Over the years, however, Microsoft Word and other word processors have become desktop publishing applications in their own right. Now you can even create a Web page with Word.

Part VI explains advanced formatting techniques in Word 2000. If you're in charge of the company newsletter, or you need to post a page on the company Intranet or create a Web page to describe your exploits on the Internet, check out the entries in this part.

In this part . . .

- ✔ Changing the color of text
- ✔ Designing Web pages
- ✔ Adding borders, shading, lines, shapes, and drop caps
- ✔ Working with text boxes, graphics, and other objects on pages
- ✔ Placing pictures and graphics in your documents
- ✔ Creating "landscape" documents
- ✔ Making columns and watermarks

Coloring Text

 If you're lucky enough to own or have access to a color printer, you can print text in different colors. And even if you don't own a color printer, you can change the color of text on-screen. You might do that to call attention to parts of a document or Web page, for example. Word offers 40 colors, plus white, black, and four gray shades.

To change the color of text, follow these steps:

1. Select the text.

2. Click the down arrow beside the Font Color button and click a color, black, white, or one of the four gray shades.

After you choose a color, the Font Color button changes color and becomes the color you chose. To apply the same color again, click the Font Color button without having to open the drop-down list. You can also apply colors by way of the Font Color menu in the Font dialog box. To get there, choose Format⇨Font.

To remove the color from text, select it, click the Font Color drop-down list, and choose Automatic.

Creating Your Own Web Site

 In the future, everyone will be famous for 15 minutes, and everyone will have a Web page. Looking toward the future, Word offers commands for creating a Web page from scratch, for turning a Word document into a Web page, and even for creating a *Web site,* a collection of hyperlinked Web pages.

If you create your Web page with the Web Page Wizard, you very likely will be asked where you want to place the items shown in the following figure — the title, frame, and hyperlinks. Fold down the corner of the page with the figure in case you have to come back here and see precisely what you are being asked about.

Title

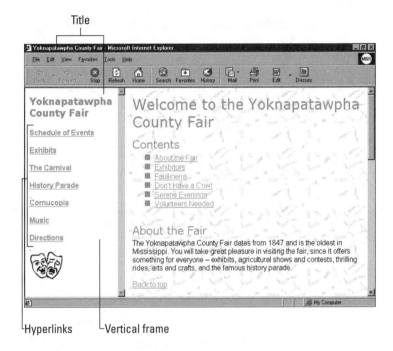

Hyperlinks ⌐Vertical frame

Creating Web pages and Web sites

Word offers three different ways to create Web pages. You can turn a Word document that you already created into a Web page; you can create a Web page from a template; or you can use the Web Page Wizard to create Web pages or even an entire Web site.

Before you create a Web page or Web site, however, you need to create a new folder in which to store it. You need the new folder because Word creates special subfolders when you create a Web page and places the subfolders in whatever folder the Web page you create is located in. The special subfolders hold support files that make displaying the Web page possible. If you disregard my advice and do not put your Web page in its own folder, you will have a hard time figuring out which files and subfolders are needed to display your Web page. When the time comes to ship your Web page files and folders to an ISP (Internet service provider) or to your network administrator so that your Web pages can be displayed on the Internet or the company network, you will not know which files and folders to send.

Converting Word documents to Web pages

A Web browser such as Internet Explorer or Netscape Navigator cannot "see" images and text or display them on a computer screen unless the images and text have been tagged with *hypertext markup language* (HTML) codes. Fortunately for you and for the teeming multitudes who will admire your Web pages, Word has made the dreary task of entering HTML codes very easy: Word can do it for you. It can code a document and do a good job of it, as long as you thoughtfully assign styles to the different parts of the document. When Word converts a document to HTML, it converts styles to HTML codes. ***See also*** "Applying Styles for Consistent Formatting" in Part III to learn about styles.

However, not all Word styles can be converted to HTML codes. Text effects, drop caps, text boxes and autoshapes, margins, page borders, footnotes and endnotes, and columns are not on speaking terms with HTML. And to convert Word documents to Web pages, Microsoft Internet Explorer must have been installed on your computer.

To turn a Word document into a Web page:

1. Open the document to be converted to an HTML document.

2. Choose File⇨Save as Web Page.

3. In the Save As dialog box, find the folder that will hold your HTML file and enter a name in the File Name box.

4. Click the Change Title button and, in the Set Page Title dialog box, enter a descriptive name for your Web page and click OK. The name you enter will appear in the title bar of the Web browser when your Web page is shown online.

5. Click the Save button. Word gives the file the *.htm* extension. When next you see the file, it appears in Web Layout View.

Creating a Web page from a template

You can save a lot of time by creating Web pages from templates. Instead of doing the layout work yourself, you can let Word do it for you. After you have created a new folder to hold your Web page, follow these steps to create a Web page from a template:

1. Choose File⇨New to open the New dialog box.

2. Click the Web Pages tab. You see several template icons. Click a couple of icons and look in the Preview box to get a glimpse of the Web pages you can create.

3. Click the template you want and click OK.

You get a generic Web page with sample text and perhaps a placeholder graphic. Your job now, if you choose to accept it, is to replace the generic text with your own words. You can call on all the formatting commands in Word, import clip art, and do what you will to make this Web page a lively one.

Creating a Web site with the Web Page Wizard

To create a Web site, a bunch of linked Web pages on the same topic, you can use the Web Page Wizard. Use the Wizard to create Web pages from scratch and also to make Web pages that you already created part of a Web site. Before you create your Web site, create a new folder to store it in. Then follow these steps to create your Web site:

1. Choose File⇨New.

2. Click the Web Pages tab in the New dialog box.

3. Double-click the Web Page Wizard icon. After a moment, you see the first Web Page Wizard dialog box. To create your Web site, you visit each Wizard dialog box — Title and Location, Navigation, Add Pages, Organize Pages, and Visual Theme — and tell Word what you want to appear on your Web site.

4. Click the Next button to go from page to page in the Web Page Wizard dialog box, answer the questions, and click the Finish button when you are done. If you change your mind while you are giving birth to your Web site, click a page name or the Back button to return to a page you visited before.

Answer the questions on these pages in the Web Page Wizard dialog box:

✦ **Title and Location:** Enter a title for the Web site and choose the folder you will store it in — the folder you created before you began developing your Web site. The title you enter appears prominently at the top of the table of contents page and in the title bar of the Web browser with which others view your site, so choose a title carefully. Click the Browse button, locate and select the folder in the Copy dialog box, and click the Open button.

✦ **Navigation:** For the *home page,* the first page that visitors see when they come to your site, choose the kind of frame you want, Vertical Frame or Horizontal Frame, or choose Separate Page for displaying only hyperlinks on the home page. This dialog box is for choosing how visitors to your site will go from page to page. As the dialog box shows, Vertical Frame places hyperlinks on the left side, Horizontal Frame places them along the top, and Separate Page places them in the middle of the home page.

♦ **Add Pages:** How many pages does your Web site need? Most Web site developers believe that no page should be so long that you have to scroll to get to the bottom. Better to divide the material across several pages.

To add a page, click the Add New Blank Page button. To include a page that you already created in the site, click the Add Existing File button, find and select the page in the Open dialog box, and click the Open button. To get a page from a template, click the Add Template Page button, choose a template in the Web Page Templates dialog box, and click OK.

♦ **Organize Pages:** If necessary, change the position of the Web pages by clicking a page and then clicking the Move Up or Move Down button.

The page at the top of the list is your home page. In navigation frames, hyperlinks to pages 2, 3, and so on appear one below the other on the left side of the screen if you choose a vertical frame, or to the right of one another along the top of the page if you choose a horizontal frame.

♦ **Visual Theme:** This is where you decide what your Web site will look like. Click the Add a Visual Theme option button, click the Browse Themes button, choose a theme for your Web pages from the Theme dialog box, and click OK. *See also* "Choosing backgrounds and themes for Web pages," the next section, to find out precisely how this dialog box works.

When you are done creating your shell of a Web site, start entering text. Go to it. The hyperlinks and design are already set up for you. Now, as they say in the business, you have to "provide the content." Visit the various pages in your Web site and enter the text and graphics.

Choosing backgrounds and themes for Web pages

To decorate your Web page, you can give it a background color or what Microsoft calls a "theme" — a coordinated design with different colors assigned to headings, text, bulleted lists, and hyperlinks. You are hereby encouraged to experiment with backgrounds and themes until you hit paydirt and fashion a lively design.

To select a background color, choose Format➪Background and select a color from the Color menu, or else click the Fill Effects option and choose a background from the Fill Effects dialog box. The Texture tab offers some neat backgrounds that are highly suitable for Web pages. To remove a background, choose Format➪ Background and click the No Fill option.

Follow these steps to choose a theme:

1. Choose Format⇨Theme. You see the Theme dialog box.

2. In the Choose a Theme list, click a few names until you see a theme you like. The Sample of Theme box shows what the themes look like.

3. Check and uncheck the Vivid Colors, Active Graphics, and Background Image check boxes in the lower-left corner of the dialog box and watch what happens in the Sample of Theme box. By checking or unchecking these check boxes, you can customize the theme.

4. Click OK.

Seeing your Web page in a browser

Choose File⇨Web Page Preview to see what your Web page looks like to someone viewing it with a Web browser. Microsoft's Web browser, Internet Explorer, opens, and you see your Web page in all its glory. A Web page as seen in Web Layout view in Word and the same page in Internet Explorer look remarkably alike.

Hyperlinking your Web page to other pages

A *hyperlink* is an electronic shortcut from one Web page to another on the Internet, from one place to another in the same Web site, or from one place to another on the same Web page. You can always tell when the pointer has moved over a hyperlink because it changes into a gloved hand with a pointing finger. And when the pointer is over a hyperlink, a box appears with either the name of the link or its address.

If you want to link your Web page to a page on the Internet, go to the page and jot down its address. You can find the address by looking in your browser's Address bar (right-click the main menu and choose Address Bar from the shortcut menu to see the Address bar in Internet Explorer). Word offers a couple techniques for entering Web addresses without typing them in, but those techniques fall in the "more trouble than its worth" category.

Word makes it very easy to create a link to a different place on the same Web page if the place happens to be a heading. If you want to link to a graphic or a place in the text, create a bookmark there (*see also* "Bookmarks for Hopping Around" in Part V).

Follow these steps to create a hyperlink on your Web page:

1. Select the text or graphic that will comprise the link. In other words, drag the pointer over the word or words that will form the hyperlink. If a graphic will comprise the hyperlink, click to select it.

2. Choose Insert⇨Hyperlink, press Ctrl+K, or right-click and choose Hyperlink. You see the Insert Hyperlink dialog box.

3. Click the ScreenTip button and, in the Set Hyperlink ScreenTip dialog box, enter a brief two- or three-word description of the hyperlink and click OK. When visitors to your site move their mouse pointers over the link, they will see the description you enter. If you don't enter a ScreenTip description, visitors merely see the address of or path to the hyperlink destination.

4. Create the link to a Web page on the Internet, another page on your Web site, or a place on the same page. If you've linked to the place you want to link to before, simply click the Inserted Link button and choose the link from the list.

- **The Internet:** Click the Existing File or Web Page button. Then type the address of the site you want to link to in the Type the File or Web Page Name text box; click the Browsed Pages button, scroll the list of sites, and click a site name (the names come from the list of sites that Internet Explorer keeps in the History folder); or click the Web Page button, go on the Internet, and find the page you want to link to make its name appear in the Type the File or Web Page Name text box.

- **Another page on the site:** Click the Existing File or Web Page button. Then click the File button, find and select the page in the Link to File dialog box, and click OK. You can also click the Recent Files button and search through the exhaustive list of the million files you opened and try to find the page there.

- **Place on the same page:** Click the Place in This Document button. Then click the plus signs next to the Headings and the Bookmarks label to see the headings and bookmarks on the page, find the one you want to link to, and click it.

5. Click OK to close the Insert Hyperlink dialog box.

 After you create a hyperlink, be sure to test it. If the link takes you to an address on the Internet, clicking the link starts the Internet Explorer browser. You soon see the page whose address you entered in the Insert Hyperlink dialog box. If the link is inside your Web site, you see the Web toolbar after you click your hyperlink. Click the Back button on the toolbar to return from whence you came.

If the hyperlink doesn't work, right-click it and choose Hyperlink⇨Edit Hyperlink. You see the Edit Hyperlink dialog box, which offers the same options as the Insert Hyperlink dialog box. Very likely, your hyperlink doesn't work because you entered it incorrectly or you linked to a page on the Internet that no longer exists. Either edit your hyperlink or reenter it.

To remove a hyperlink, right-click it and choose Hyperlink⇨ Remove Hyperlink.

Decorating a Page with a Border

 Word offers a means of decorating title pages, certificates, menus, and similar documents with a page border. Besides lines, you can decorate the sides of a page with stars, pieces of cake, and other artwork. If you want to place a border around a page in the middle of the document, you must create a section break where the page is. Here's how to put borders around a page:

1. Place the cursor on the first page of a document if you want to put a border around only the first page. If your document is divided in sections and you want to put borders around certain pages in a section, place the cursor in the section, either the first page, if you want the borders to go around it, or in a subsequent page.

2. Choose Format⇨Borders and Shading.

3. Click the Page Border tab.

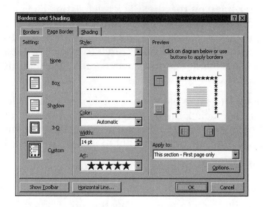

4. Under Setting, choose which kind of border you want. The Custom setting is for putting borders on one, two, or three sides of the page, not four. Use the None setting to remove borders.

5. Under Style, scroll down the list and choose a line for the borders. You will find interesting choices at the bottom of the menu. Be sure to look in the Preview window to see what your choices in this dialog box add up to.

6. Click the Color drop-down list and choose a color for the borderlines if you want a color border and you have a color printer.

7. If you chose artwork for the borders, use the Width drop-down list to tell Word how wide the lines or artwork should be.

8. Click the Art drop-down list and choose a symbol, illustration, star, piece of cake, or other artwork, if that is what you want for the borders. You will find some amusing choices on this long list, including ice cream cones, bats, and umbrellas.

9. Use the four buttons in the Preview window to tell Word on which sides of the page you want borders. Click these buttons to remove or add borders, as you wish.

10. Under Apply To, tell Word which page or pages in the document get borders.

11. Click the Options button and fill in the Border and Shading Options dialog box if you want to get specific about how close the borders can come to the edge of the page or pages.

12. Click OK.

Drawing Lines and Shapes

The Drawing toolbar offers many opportunities for decorating documents and Web pages with lines, lines with arrows on the end, shapes such as ovals and rectangles, and what Word calls *autoshapes* — stars, banners, and various other artistic tidbits. You can even create shadow backgrounds and 3-D effects for shapes. This figure shows some of the things you can do with the buttons and menus on the Drawing toolbar:

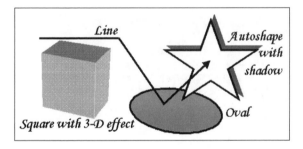

Follow these steps to draw lines and shapes:

1. Display the Drawing toolbar. To do so, click the Drawing button on the Standard toolbar, or right-click a toolbar and choose Drawing from the shortcut menu.

2. Click the appropriate button on the Drawing toolbar and then drag the pointer across the screen to draw the line or shape.

See also "Handling Objects on Pages" later in Part VI to find out how to shrink or enlarge lines and shapes, move them, fill them with color, and change the width of lines on their borders.

Here are the specifics of drawing lines and shapes:

✦ **Drawing lines:** Click the Line button and drag the pointer across the screen to draw the line.

✦ **Drawing arrows on lines:** Start by clicking the Line or Arrow button and drawing a line. To choose an arrow style of your own, select the line by clicking it, click the Arrow Style button, and choose a style from the pop-up menu. Choose More Arrows from the pop-up menu to go to the Format AutoShape dialog box and select different arrows or different-size arrows for either side of the line.

✦ **Drawing rectangles and ovals:** Click the Rectangle or Oval button and drag the cursor across the screen to draw the rectangle or oval. Hold down the Shift key as you drag to draw a square or circle.

✦ **Drawing an autoshape:** Click the AutoShapes button, move the pointer over a submenu, and click a shape. Then drag the cursor across the screen to draw it. A yellow diamond appears beside some autoshapes so that you can adjust their appearance. Drag the yellow diamond to make the autoshape look just right. The AutoShapes submenus offer many different shapes.

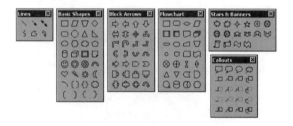

✦ **Putting shadows and three-dimensional effects on shapes:** Click a shape, click the Shadow or 3-D button, and choose shadow style or 3-D effect from the pop-up menu. Choose No Shadow or No 3-D to remove shadows and third dimensions.

Experiment with the buttons and menus on the Drawing toolbar. Personally, I am very fond of the Callouts options on the AutoShapes menu of the Drawing toolbar because I can make use of them along with Word's clip art files to fool people into thinking that I am a real cartoonist.

Dropping In a Drop Cap

A *drop cap* is a large capital letter that "drops" into the text. Drop caps appear at the start of chapters in antiquated books, but you can find other uses for them. Here, a drop cap marks the "A" side of a list of songs on a homemade reggae tape.

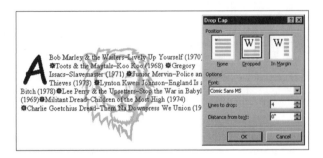

To create a drop cap:

1. Click anywhere in the paragraph whose first letter you want to "drop."

2. Choose Format⇨Drop Cap.

3. In the Drop Cap dialog box, choose which kind of drop cap you want by clicking a box. The None setting is for removing a drop cap.

4. Choose a font from the Font drop-down list. Choose one that's different from the text in the paragraph. You can come back to this dialog box and get a different font later, if you wish.

5. In the Lines to Drop scroll box, choose how many text lines the letter should "drop on."

6. Keep the 0 setting in the Distance from Te**x**t box unless you're dropping an *I, 1,* or other skinny letter or number.

7. Click OK.

You see your drop cap in Print Layout View. The drop cap appears in a text frame. To change the size of the drop cap, you can tug and pull at the sides of the box (by dragging the handles with the mouse). However, you're better off choosing Format⇨Drop Cap again and playing with the settings in the Drop Cap dialog box.

Fixing Spacing Problems in Headings

Sometimes when you enlarge text for a heading, one or two letters in the words end up being too close together or too far apart. For example, in the following heading, the *T* and *W* in *TWINS* are too far apart, as are the *Y*s and *O*s in *YO-YOS* and the *O* and *S* in *LOST.* I fixed this problem by kerning the letter pairs. *Kerning* means to adjust the amount of space between two letters.

```
TWINS' YO-YOS LOST!
TWINS' YO-YOS LOST!
```

Follow these steps to kern a letter pair and make a large heading easier to read:

1. Select the two letters that are too far apart or too close together.

2. Choose Format⇨Font or press Ctrl+D.

3. Click the Cha**r**acter Spacing tab in the Font dialog box.

4. In the **S**pacing menu, choose Expanded to spread the letters out or Condensed to pack them in.

5. Word changes the number in the **B**y box for you, but you can do yet more packing or spreading by clicking the down or up arrow yourself. Watch the Preview box to see how close or far apart you have made the letters.

6. Click the **K**erning for Fonts check box and enter a point size in the P**o**ints and Above box if you want Word to kern fonts above a certain point size automatically.

7. Click OK.

Handling Objects on Pages

After you place a clip art image, graphic, text box, line, shape, autoshape, or WordArt image in a document, it ceases being what it was before and becomes a mere object, at least as far as Word is concerned. That's good news, however, because the techniques for manipulating objects are the same. To move, reshape, draw borders around, fill in, lock in place, overlap, or wrap text around an object, use the techniques described on the following pages.

Selecting objects

Before you can do anything to an object, you have to select it. To do so, click the object. You can tell when an object has been selected because square *selection handles* appear on the sides and corners (in lines, only two selection handles appear, one on either side of the line). To select more than one object at the same time, hold down the Shift key and click the objects.

When objects overlap, sometimes selecting one of them is difficult. To select an object that is stuck among other objects, click the Select Objects button on the Drawing toolbar and then click the object.

Moving and resizing graphics, text boxes, and other objects

Moving an object on a page is easy enough. All you have to do is click the graphic, text box, shape, or whatever, wait till you see the four-headed arrow, and click. Next, drag the pointer where you want the object to be on the page. Dotted lines show where you are moving the object. When the object is in the right position, release the mouse button. If you are moving a text box, place the pointer on the perimeter of the box to see the four-headed arrow.

If you can't move an object, it's because Word thinks that it is an inline image and shouldn't be moved. On the Picture toolbar, click the Text Wrapping button and click any button on the pop-up menu except Edit Wrap Points. *See also* "Wrapping text around a text box, graphic, or other object" later in this part if you need to know how text wrapping works.

How you change an object's size depends on whether you want to keep its proportions:

+ **Changing size but not proportions:** To change the size of an object but keep its proportions, click the object and move the cursor to one of the selection handles on the *corners*. The cursor changes into a double-headed arrow. Click and start dragging. Dotted lines show how you are changing the size of the frame. When it's the right size, release the mouse button.

✦ **Changing size and proportions:** To change both the size of an object *and* its proportions, move the cursor to a selection handle on the *side*. When the cursor changes into a double-headed arrow, click and start dragging. Dotted lines show how the object is being changed. When it is the size and shape you want, release the mouse button.

This illustration shows the same graphic at three different sizes. The original graphic is on the left. For the middle graphic, I pulled a corner selection handle to enlarge it but keep its proportions. For the one on the right, I pulled a selection handle on the side to enlarge it and change its proportions.

 If you want to get very specific about how big an object is, go to the Size tab of the Format dialog box. To do that, right-click the object, choose Format, and click the Size tab. Then enter measurements in the Height and Width boxes. Go this route if you want to make text boxes or graphics the same size, for example.

Borders and color shades for graphics, text boxes, and other objects

By putting borders around graphics, text boxes, shapes, and other objects, and by putting interesting gray shades and colors behind them as well, you can amuse yourself on a rainy afternoon. And you can sometimes create fanciful artwork. These text boxes and graphics were created by a 7-year-old with help from his father. This part of the book explains how to put borders and gray shades on objects.

Putting borders on objects

The fastest way to put a border around an object is to select it, click the Line Style button on the Picture or Drawing toolbar, and choose a line from the pop-up menu. To change the color of borders, click the down arrow beside the Line Color button on the Drawing toolbar and then choose a color from the pop-up menu.

To get fancy with borders, click the object and do the following:

1. Right-click the object and choose Format from the shortcut menu, or else choose F̲ormat on the menu bar and then choose the bottom-most command on the F̲ormat menu. Which command that is — P̲icture, O̲bject, Text B̲ox, or Aut̲oShape — depends on what kind of object you are working on.

2. Click the Colors and Lines tab in the Format dialog box. (You can also get here by clicking the Line Style button on the Drawing or Picture toolbar and choosing M̲ore Lines.)

3. Under Line, click the C̲olor drop-down list and choose a color. (Black is the first choice in the box.) Click the No Line option to remove borders from an object.

4. Click the D̲ashed down arrow and choose a dashed or dotted line, if you want.

5. Click the S̲tyle down arrow and tell Word what kind of line you want. You find exotic choices at the bottom of the menu.

6. Click arrows in the W̲eight box or enter a number yourself to tell Word how wide or narrow to make the borderlines.

7. Click OK.

Filling an object with a color or gray shade

The fast way to "fill" a graphic or text box is to select it, click the down arrow beside the Fill Color button on the Drawing toolbar, and choose a color or gray shade. By clicking F̲ill Effects at the bottom of the menu, you can get to interesting gray shades and textures.

Or, if you are the kind who likes dialog boxes, select the thing you are filling and either right-click and choose Format, or else choose F̲ormat on the menu bar and then choose the bottom-most command on the Format menu — Picture, Object, Text Box, or AutoShape. Then click the Colors and Lines tab in the Format dialog box, click the Color drop-down list, and make a choice. Experiment with the Semitransparent check box if you want a soupy, fainter-looking color.

Locking objects in place

Suppose that you want an object such as a text box, WordArt image, or clip art image to stay in the same place. Normally, what is in the middle of page 1 is pushed to the bottom of the page or to page 2 when you insert paragraphs at the start of a document. What if you want the paragraph or graphic to stay put, come hell or high water? In that case, you can *lock* it to the page. After you lock it, text flows around your image or text box, but the image or text box stays put. Follow these steps to lock an object in place:

1. Move the object to the position on the page where you want it to remain at all times.

2. Right-click the object or select the object, choose Format, and then choose the last command on the format menu. (The command is named after the kind of object you are working with.)

3. Click the Layout tab in the Format dialog box.

4. On the Layout tab, choose any Wrapping Style option; however, you can't choose In Line with Text if the In Line with Text option is selected. *See also* "Wrapping text around a text box, graphic, or other object" later in this part to find out about text wrapping.

5. Click the Advanced button.

6. In the Advanced Layout dialog box, click the Picture Position tab.

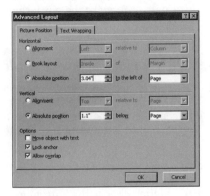

7. Click the Absolute Position option button under Vertical.

8. Click the Lock Anchor check box.

9. Click the Move Object with Text check box to remove the check mark. As soon as you do so, the Absolute Position Below setting under Vertical changes to Page.

10. Under Horizontal, choose Page from the Absolute <u>P</u>osition <u>T</u>o the Left Of drop-down list. Now the object is locked, horizontally and vertically, to the page, and Word knows to keep it at its current position on the page and *not* move it in the document when text is inserted before it. For now, don't worry about the To the Left Of and Below settings. In Step 12, you will drag the object on the page exactly where you want it to be.

11. Click OK in the Advanced Layout dialog box and OK again in the Format dialog box. Back in your document, your object may have slid to a different position.

12. Drag the object where you want it to be on the page.

 To tell whether an object has been locked in place, click the Show/Hide ¶ button and look for the picture of an anchor and a tiny padlock in the left margin of the document. ***See also*** "Wrapping text around a text box, graphic, or other object" later in this part to tell Word what nearby text should do when it bumps up against an object.

Handling objects that overlap

Chances are, objects like the ones in this figure overlap when more than one appears on the same page. And when objects are placed beside text, do you want the text to appear in front of the objects, or do you want the objects to cover up the text?

Word offers special Order commands for determining how objects overlap with one another and with text. However, before you know anything about the Order commands, you need to know about *layers,* also known as *drawing layers.* From top to bottom, text and objects can appear on these layers:

✦ **Foreground layer:** Objects on this layer cover up objects on the text layer and background layer. Only objects, not text, can appear on the foreground layer. When you insert a new object in a document, it appears on the foreground layer.

✦ **Text layer:** The text you type appears on this layer. No objects can appear on this layer. Text on this layer is covered by objects on the foreground layer but covers objects on the background layer.

+ **Background layer:** Only objects can appear on this layer. Objects on the background layer are covered by objects on the foreground layer and by text.

Follow these steps to tell Word whether an object should overlap text or overlap other objects:

1. Click the object to select it.

2. Click the D<u>r</u>aw button on the Drawing toolbar, choose <u>O</u>rder, and choose a Send or Bring command on the Order menu; or right-click, choose O<u>r</u>der, and choose a submenu command.

The commands on the Order submenu do the following:

+ **Bring to Front:** When objects are on the same layer, either the foreground or background, moves the object in front of all others on the layer.

+ **Send to Back:** When objects are on the same layer, moves the object behind all others on the layer.

+ **Bring Forward:** When three or more objects are on the same layer, either foreground or background, moves the object higher in the stack of objects.

+ **Send Backward:** When three or more objects are on the same layer, moves the object lower in the stack so that more objects overlap the object you selected.

+ **Bring in Front of Text:** Moves the object from the background layer to the foreground layer, where it appears in front of text.

+ **Send Behind Text:** Moves the object from the foreground layer to the background layer, where it appears behind text.

Wrapping text around a text box, graphic, or other object

Word gives you lots of interesting opportunities to wrap text around text boxes, graphics, and other objects in a document. By playing with the different ways to wrap text, you can create very sophisticated layouts. When you wrap text, you pick a wrapping style and the side of the object around which to wrap the text. This figure demonstrates several of the wrapping styles and directions that text can be wrapped.

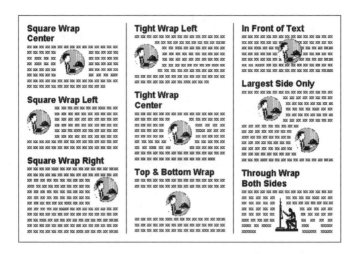

 The fastest way to wrap text is to click the object around which text is to be wrapped, click the Text Wrapping button on the Picture toolbar, and choose an option from the drop-down list.

 Wrapped text looks best when it is justified and hyphenated. That way, text can get closer to the object that is being wrapped.

To wrap text around an object:

1. Select the object by clicking it.

2. Right-click and choose Format, or else choose Format on the menu bar and then choose the last option on the Format menu. (The option is named after the kind of object you are dealing with.)

3. Click the Layout tab in the Format dialog box.

4. Click a box under Wrapping Style to tell Word how you want the text to behave when it reaches the graphic or text box. The In Line with Text option keeps text from wrapping around objects.

5. Under Horizontal Alignment, tell Word where you want the object to be in relation to the text. For example, click the Left radio button to make the object stand to the left side of text as it flows down the page.

If you want text to wrap to the largest side or to both sides without the object being centered, click the Other radio button and then click the Advanced button. In the Advanced Layout dialog box, click the Text Wrapping tab, choose either the Both Sides or Largest Only radio button, and click OK. The Text Wrapping tab also offers choices for telling Word how close text can come to the object as it wraps around it.

6. Click OK.

Inserting Pictures and Graphics in Documents

If you keep clip art on your computer, and as long as the Word 2000 CD is sitting in your CD-ROM drive, you have a golden opportunity to embellish your documents with art created by genuine artists. You don't have to tell anyone where this art came from, either, as long as you are a good liar.

This entry explains how to insert a clip art image, change its resolutions, and crop it. *See also* "Handling Objects on Pages" earlier in this part to find out how to move and change the size and shape of a clip art image, put borders and color shades on it, or wrap text around it.

Inserting a clip art image

Before you insert a clip art image, make sure that the Word 2000 CD is loaded in your computer. Word gets images from the CD. Then follow these steps to insert a clip art image:

1. Click in the paragraph that you want the image to be attached to. As the paragraph moves from page to page during editing, so will your image, so choose a paragraph carefully.

2. Click the Insert Clip Art button on the Drawing toolbar or choose Insert⇨Picture⇨Clip Art. You see the Insert ClipArt dialog box.

3. Find the clip art image that you want to insert. In the course of your search, you can click the Back or Forward button to retrace your steps or return to images you saw before.

- **Search by keyword:** In the Search for Clips text box, type a word that describes what kind of clip art you want, and press Enter. You can choose a keyword from the drop-down list if you are reenacting a keyword search that you made earlier.

- **Scroll to a category and select it:** Scroll through the category list and click a category that piques your interest. Click the All Categories button (or press Alt+Home) to see all the categories again if that proves necessary.

- **Scrounge images from the Internet:** Click the Clips Online button and follow the directions to go to Microsoft's Clip Gallery Live site. When you get there, either enter a keyword for the search or search by category from the Browse drop-down list. To download an image to your computer, check it off, click it, and then click its larger preview image. The image appears in the Insert ClipArt dialog box. Images scrounged from the Internet are kept in the Downloaded Clips category of the Insert ClipArt dialog box.

4. When you've found the image you want, click it. A callout menu appears. You can click the Preview Clip button on the callout menu to get a better look at your images.

5. Click the Insert Clip button to place the image in your document.

You can insert a graphic by clicking the Insert Picture button on the Picture toolbar or by choosing Insert⇨Picture⇨From File and, in the Insert Picture dialog box, finding and double-clicking the name of the graphic file whose image you want to insert.

Experimenting with brightness, contrast, and appearance

After you have inserted an image, you can alter it a bit by experimenting with its brightness and contrast or by turning it into a grayscale or black-and-white image. Here's how:

1. Click the image to select it. You know that an image is selected when its square selection handles appear.

2. Display the Picture toolbar and experiment with the different buttons:

 • **Image Control:** Click the Image Control button and choose <u>G</u>rayscale to see the image in shades of gray, <u>B</u>lack & White to see the *film noir* version, or <u>W</u>atermark to see a bleached-out image.

 • **More Contrast and Less Contrast:** These buttons either heighten or mute line and color distinctions.

 • **More Brightness and Less Brightness:** These buttons either lighten or darken the image.

 To get the original picture back if you experiment too enthusiastically, either click the Reset Picture button on the Picture toolbar or click the Image Control button and choose Automatic.

 You can also experiment with clip art images by clicking the Format Picture button on the Picture toolbar or by choosing Format⇨Picture. On the Picture tab of the Format Picture dialog box, choose an option from the Color menu or use the Brightness and Contrast sliders to alter your image. However, you can't see how good an artist you are until you click OK and view your image on-screen.

For the image on the left, I chose 33% brightness, 66% contrast; for the one to its right, 50% brightness, 50% contrast; and for the one to its right, 66% brightness, 33% contrast. The image on the far right is a watermark.

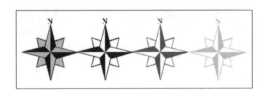

Cropping off part of a graphic

You can *crop* — that is, cut off parts of — a graphic, but not very elegantly. To do that, select a graphic and click the Crop button on the Picture toolbar. The pointer changes into an odd shape with two intersecting triangles on it. Move the pointer to a selection handle and start dragging. The dotted line tells you what part of a graphic you are cutting off. Sorry, you can crop off only the sides of a graphic. You can't cut a circle out of the middle, for example, proving once again that the computer will never replace that ancient and noble device, the scissors.

Landscape Documents

A *landscape* document is one in which the page is wider than it is long, like a painting of a landscape. Most documents, like the pages of this book, are printed in *portrait* style, with the short sides of the page on the top and bottom. However, creating a landscape document is sometimes a good idea because a landscape document stands out from the usual crowd of portrait documents. Create a new section for your landscape page if you want to place it in a document of portrait pages.

To turn the page on its ear and create a landscape document, follow these steps:

1. Choose File⇨Page Setup.

2. Click the Paper Size tab.

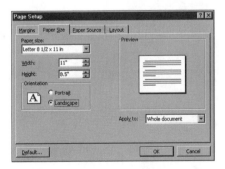

3. In the Orientation area, click the Landscape option button. The piece of paper in the Preview box turns on its side.

4. In the Apply To box, choose Whole Document to print landscape pages throughout the document, This Section to print only the section the cursor is in, or This Point Forward to make the rest of the pages in the document landscape pages.

5. Click OK.

See also "Printing on Different-Sized Paper," in Part IV, to learn other ways of creating documents on different paper sizes and shapes.

Making Room to Bind a Document

If you intend to bind a document, you need to make room for the binding. Big plastic bindings eat into page margins and make the text beside the binding difficult to read. Lucky for you, Word makes handling bindings easy:

1. Choose File⇨Page Setup.

2. On the Margins tab, click the up arrow beside the Gutter box. As you do so, watch the Preview box to see how the binding eats into your document.

3. If yours is a two-sided document with text printed on both sides of the paper, click the Mirror Margins check box and adjust the gutter accordingly.

4. Now that you can see how big the gutter is in the dialog box, adjust the Left or Inside Margin setting. In a document in which text is printed on both sides of the paper, the inside margin is the one closest to the binding.

5. Click OK.

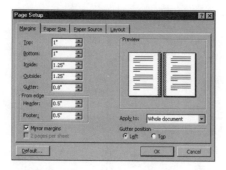

Putting Newspaper-Style Columns in a Document

Columns look great in newsletters and similar documents. And you can pack a lot of words in columns. With columns, you can present more than one document on a single page so that readers have a choice of what they read.

Before you put text in newspaper-style columns, write it. Take care of the spelling, grammar, and everything else first because making text changes to words after they've been arranged in columns is hard.

Sometimes it is easier to create columns by creating a table or by using tabs instead, especially when the columns refer to one another. In a two-column résumé, for example, the left-hand column often lists job titles ("Facsimile Engineer") whose descriptions are found directly across the page in the right-hand column ("I photocopied stuff all day long"). Creating a two-column résumé with Word's Format⇨Columns command would be futile because making the columns line up is impossible. Each time you add something to the left-hand column, everything "snakes" — it gets bumped down in the left-hand column and the right-hand column as well.

There are two ways to create columns: with the Columns button on the toolbar and with the Format⇨Columns command. Format⇨Columns gives you considerably more leeway because the Columns button lets you create only columns of equal width. To use the Columns button:

1. Select the text to be put in columns or simply place the cursor in the document to "columnize" all the text.

2. Click the Columns button on the toolbar. A menu drops down so that you can choose how many columns you want.

3. Click and drag to choose from one to six columns.

Word creates a new section if you selected text before you columnized it, and you see your columns in Print Layout View. Very likely, they don't look so good. It's hard to get it right the first time. You can drag the column border bars on the ruler to widen or narrow the columns:

Drag to change column width.

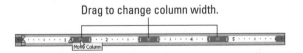

However, it's much easier to choose Format⇨Columns and play with options in the Columns dialog box. If you want to start all over, or if you want to start from the beginning with the Columns dialog box, here's how:

1. Select the text to be put in columns, or put the cursor in the section to be put in columns, or place the cursor at a position in the document where columns are to start appearing.

2. Choose Format⇨Columns.

3. Choose options from the Columns dialog box. As you do so, keep your eye on the Preview box in the lower-right corner:

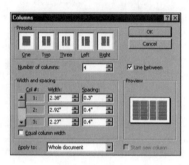

• **Presets:** Click a box to choose a preset number of columns. Notice that, in some of the boxes, the columns aren't of equal width. Choose One if you want to remove columns from a document.

• **Number of Columns:** If you want more than three columns, enter a number here.

• **Line Between:** Click this box to put lines between columns.

• **Col #:** If your document has more than three columns, a scroll bar appears to the left of the Col # boxes. Scroll to the column you want to work with.

• **Width:** If you click the Equal Column Width box to remove the check mark, you can make columns of unequal width. Change the width of each column by using the Width boxes.

• **Spacing:** Determines how much blank space appears to the right of the column.

• **Equal Column Width:** Click this box to remove the check mark if you want columns of various widths.

• **Apply To:** Choose which part of the document you want to "columnize" — selected text, the section the cursor is in, this point forward in your document, or the whole document.

• **Start New Column:** This box is for putting empty space in a column, perhaps to insert a text box or picture. Place the cursor where you want the empty space to begin, open the Columns dialog box, click this check box, and choose This Point Forward from the Apply To drop-down list. Text below the cursor moves to the next column.

4. Click OK.

Faster ways to "break" a column in the middle and move text to the next column are to press Ctrl+Shift+Enter or choose Insert⇨Break and click the Column Break radio button.

As you format your multicolumn newsletter or incendiary pamphlet, click the Print Preview button early and often. The best way to see what a multicolumn document really looks like is to see it on the Print Preview screen.

Watermarking for the Elegant Effect

A *watermark* is a pale image that appears behind text on each page in a document. True watermarks are made in the paper mold and can be seen only when the sheet of paper is held up to a light. You can't make true watermarks with Word, but you can make the closest thing to them that can be attained in the debased digital world in which we live.

Strange as it may seem, you create a watermark by making it part of the header or footer. As long as the clip art image that forms the watermark is inserted along with the header or footer, it appears on every page — like a header or footer.

Follow these steps to create a watermark for every page of a document:

1. Choose View⇨Header and Footer.

2. While the Header box is open, insert a clip art image. ***See also*** "Inserting Pictures and Graphics in Documents," also in Part VI, if you need help.

3. With the header box still open, drag your clip art image onto the main part of the page. Resize it if necessary. ***See also*** "Handling Objects on Pages" earlier in Part VI.

4. Display the Picture toolbar (right-click a toolbar and choose Picture to do so).

5. Click the Image Control button on the Picture toolbar and choose Watermark from the drop-down list.

6. Click the Close button on the Header and Footer toolbar.

Choose View⇨Header and Footer and toy with the image some more if you have to adjust your watermark. When you type text, it appears on top of the watermark. This figure shows two pages of a letter in which the paper has been "watermarked."

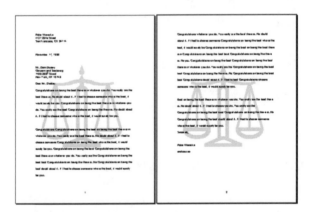

WordArt for Embellishing Documents

You can bend, spindle, and mutilate text with a feature called WordArt. I believe that this feature was inspired by old superhero comics, in which words and images that may have come from the WordArt Gallery appeared whenever Batman, Spiderman, and Wonder Woman brawled with the criminal element.

WordArt, a memory hog, makes computers run very slowly. Don't experiment with WordArt if you are in a hurry or your computer lacks memory.

To create a WordArt image, put the cursor roughly where you want
the image to go and do the following:

 1. Choose Insert⇨Picture⇨WordArt or click the Insert WordArt
   button on the Drawing toolbar. You see the WordArt Gallery.

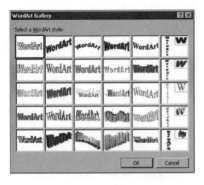

 2. Click the image that strikes your fancy and then click OK.

 3. In the Edit WordArt Text dialog box, type a word or words of
   your own.

 4. Choose a new font from the Font menu or change the size of
   letters with the Size menu, and click OK.

The image arrives on-screen with its selection handles showing. To
really bend the word or words out of shape, click and drag the
yellow diamond on the image. To change the wording, click Edit
Text on the WordArt toolbar to reopen the Edit WordArt Text
dialog box. To choose a new WordArt image, click the WordArt
Gallery button. To change the shape of a WordArt image, click the
WordArt Shape button on the WordArt toolbar and choose a shape
from the pop-up menu.

See also "Handling Objects on Pages" earlier in this part if you
need advice for moving, resizing, or otherwise manipulating
WordArt images.

Working with Text Boxes

Put text in a text box when you want it to stand out on the page.
Text boxes like the one shown here can be shaded, filled with
color, and given borders. What's more, you can move one around
at will on the page until it lands in the right place. You can even
use text boxes as columns and make text jump from one text box

to the next in a document — a nice feature, for example, when you want a newsletter article on page 1 to be continued on page 2. Instead of cutting and pasting text from page 1 to page 2, Word moves the text for you as the column on page 1 fills up.

> The building manager and the fire department will conduct a test of the fire alarms in the building on Tuesday, September 26 at 10:00. Ignore the fire alarms—unless, of course, there is a real fire.

See also "Handling Objects on Pages" in this part to find out how to change the size of a text box, change its borders, fill it with color, and move it on-screen.

Inserting a text box

To put a text box in a document, follow these steps:

1. Choose Insert⇨Text Box or click the Text Box button on the Drawing toolbar. The pointer turns into a cross.

2. Click and drag to draw the text box. Lines show you how big it will be when you release the mouse button.

3. Release the mouse button.

After you've inserted the text box, you can type text in it and call on all the formatting techniques in Word to boldface it, align it, or do what you will with it.

Changing the direction of the text

On the Text Box toolbar is a little toy called the Change Text Direction button. Click a text box and click this button to make the text in the text box change orientation. Here, you can see what happens when you click the Change Text Direction button.

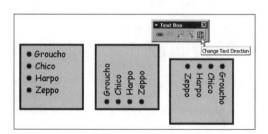

Linking the text in different text boxes

As I mention earlier, you can link text boxes so that the text in the first box is pushed into the next one when it fills up. To link text boxes, start by creating all the text boxes that you will need. You cannot link one text box to another if the second text box already has text in it. Use these buttons on the Text Box toolbar to link the text boxes in a document:

✦ **Create Text Box Link:** Click a text box and then click this button to create a forward link. When you click the button, the pointer changes into a very odd-looking pointer that is supposed to look like a pitcher. Move the odd-looking pointer to the next text box in the chain and click there to create a link.

✦ **Break Forward Link:** To break a link, click the text box that is to be the last in the chain, and then click the Break Forward Link button.

✦ **Previous Text Box and Next Text Box:** Click these buttons to go backward or forward through the text boxes in the chain.

Fancy and Esoteric Stuff

Everything in Part VII deserves a Cool Stuff icon. You find instructions here for doing tasks that would take hours and hours without Word 2000's help. Most of the tasks have to do with generating lists of one kind or another — tables of contents, tables of figures, and indexes. You also find some neat shortcuts for tracking changes to documents and writing commentary on documents.

In this part . . .

✔ **Making comments about a document**

✔ **Generating tables of figures, tables of contents, and other tables**

✔ **Creating an index**

✔ **Creating and working with captions, cross-references, footnotes, and endnotes**

✔ **Keeping track of revisions made to documents**

Commenting on a Document

In the old days, comments were scribbled illegibly in the margins of books and documents, but in Word, comments are easy to read. Where comments have been made in a document, the text is highlighted. As shown here, all you have to do is move the cursor over the highlighted text to read the comment and the name of the person who made it. (Choose Tools⇨Options, click the View tab in the Options dialog box, and check the ScreenTips option if comments aren't highlighted on your screen.)

> **Anne Crowley:**
> Re this whole paragraph: Has he gone mental?
>
> Furthermore, the unemployment rate among spies has skyrocketed since the end of the Cold War. Perfectly talented individuals—women and men capable of wire-taping a building in, say, a matter of minutes—now have anywhere to sell their services. Surely we can seek out and recruit these individuals for our own efforts. After all, industrial espionage is the only game, now that intragovernment espionage has bitten the dust.

If you are putting together a proposal, you can pass it around the office and invite everyone to comment on it. If someone makes an especially good comment, you can include it in the main text merely by copying and pasting it.

To write a comment:

1. Select the word or sentence that you want to criticize or praise.

2. Choose Insert⇨Comment. A window opens at the bottom of the screen with comments that have already been made and the initials of the people who made them. The comments are numbered.

Click to see comments by individual reviewers.

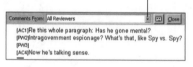

> Comments From: All Reviewers
> [AC1]Re this whole paragraph: Has he gone mental?
> [PW2]Intragovernment espionage? What's that, like Spy vs. Spy?
> [PW3]
> [AC4]Now he's talking sense.

3. Type your comment next to the square brackets with your initials in them. (If your initials don't appear in the brackets, choose Tools⇨Options, click the User Information tab, and type your initials in the Initials box.)

4. Click the Close button.

TIP

Besides placing the cursor on a highlighted comment to read it, you can read the entire list of comments by choosing View⇨ Comments. Click a comment in the Comment window, and the document window scrolls to the place in the text where the comment was made. If you are a fan of toolbars, you can display the Reviewing toolbar and click its buttons to insert, edit, delete, and go forward or backward to comments.

If a comment is so good that it belongs in the document, simply select it in the Comment window, drag it into the document, and reformat or rewrite it as necessary.

To delete a comment, right-click its highlighting in the text and choose Delete Comment from the shortcut menu. The remaining annotations are renumbered. To delete all the comments in a document, click the Show/Hide ¶ button on the Standard toolbar and choose Edit⇨Replace. In the Find and Replace dialog box, click the Format button, and choose Comment Mark from the pop-up menu. Then click the Replace All button to replace all comments in the document with what is in the Replace With text box — in other words, with nothing.

Creating a Table of Figures, Graphs, and More

A table of figures, graphs, equations, illustrations, listings, pro-grams, or tables sometimes appears at the start of technical documents and scholarly papers so that readers can refer to figures, graphs, or whatnot quickly. In Word, you can create tables of all the items in the aforementioned list. To do so, however, you must have used the Insert⇨Caption command to create the captions for the figures, graphs, and so on. (*See also* "Putting Captions on Figures and Tables" later in Part VII if you'd like Word's help with captions.)

To generate the table:

1. Put the cursor where you want the table to go.

2. Choose Insert⇨Index and Tables.

3. Click the Table of Figures tab.

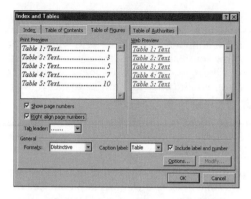

4. Choose options on the tab. As you do so, watch the Print Preview and Web Preview boxes to see how your choices affect the table's appearance. The Web Preview box shows what your table will look like if you display it as a Web page.

- **Show Page Numbers:** Includes page numbers in the table.

- **Right Align Page Numbers:** Aligns the numbers along the right side of the table so that the ones and tens line up under each other.

- **Tab Leader:** Choose another leader, or no leader at all, if you don't want a line of periods to appear between the caption and the number of the page on which it appears.

- **Formats:** Choose a format from the list if you don't want to use the one from the template.

- **Caption Label:** Choose what kind of table you're creating.

- **Include Label and Number:** Includes the word *Equation, Figure, Graph, Illustration, Listing, Program,* or *Table,* as well as the number or letter in the table caption.

- **Options:** Lets you create tables from the styles used in your document or the fields found in the tables.

- **Modify:** As long as you chose From Template in the Formats list, you can modify the template's table format by clicking the Modify button and creating a new table style of your own. ***See also*** "Applying Styles for Consistent Formatting" in Part III to see how to create a new style.

5. Click OK when you're done.

To update your table of figures, graphs, or whatnots, right-click it and choose Update Field from the shortcut menu. Then choose Update Page Numbers Only to update the page numbers in the table as it stands now or Update Entire Table to regenerate the table so that it includes new figures, graphs, or whatever. By clicking an entry in the table, you can go directly to the thing it refers to in the document. What's more, the Web toolbar appears on-screen. Click the Back or Forward button on the Web toolbar to leap backward and forward to and from the table you created and the figures, graphs, or whatnots in your document.

Generating a Table of Contents

A book-size document isn't worth very much without a table of contents (TOC). How else can readers find what they're looking for? Generating a table of contents with Word is easy, as long as you give the headings in the document different styles — Heading 1, Heading 2, and so on. *See also* "Applying Styles for Consistent Formatting" in Part III to learn about styles.

Before you create your TOC, create a new section in which to put it and number the pages in the new section with Roman numerals. TOCs, including the TOC in this book, are usually numbered in this way. The first entry in the TOC should cite page number 1. If you don't take my advice to create a new section, the TOC will occupy the first few numbered pages of your document, and the number scheme will be thrown off. *See also* "Dividing a Document into Sections" in Part III and "Numbering the Pages" in Part II.

To create a table of contents:

1. Place the cursor where you want the TOC to go.

2. Choose Insert⇨Index and Tables.

3. Click the Table of Contents tab in the Index and Tables dialog box.

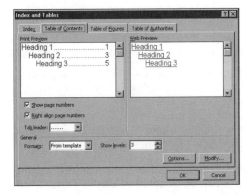

4. Choose options in the dialog box. As you do so, watch the Print Preview and Web Preview boxes to see what effect your choices have.

5. Click OK when you're done.

The Table of Contents tab gives you several ways to control what goes in your TOC and what it looks like:

✦ **Show Page Numbers:** Uncheck this box if you want your TOC to be a simple list that doesn't refer to headings by page.

✦ **Right Align Page Numbers:** Aligns the page numbers along the right side of the TOC so that the ones and tens line up under each other.

✦ **Tab Leader:** A *leader* is the punctuation mark that appears between the heading and the page number that the heading is on. If you don't want periods as the leader, choose another leader or choose (none).

✦ **Formats:** Choose a format from the list if you don't care to use the one from the template.

✦ **Show Levels:** Determines how many heading levels are included in the TOC. Unless your document is a legal contract or other formal paper, enter a **2** or **3** here. A TOC is supposed to help readers find information quickly. Including lots of headings that take a long time to read through defeats the purpose of having a TOC.

✦ **Options**: Opens the Table of Contents Options dialog box so that you can create TOC entries from the styles in your document. Click this button if you've created a Chapter Title style, for example. Scroll down the TOC Level box to find the style you want to include, and type a level number in the box beside its name. Chapter titles should be given the 1 level. You can also include text in fields in the TOC by clicking the Table Entry Fields check box. Index entries and tables of figures, for example, can be included in the TOC with this check box. Click Reset if you get all tangled up and want to start over.

✦ **Modify:** Click this button and then click the Modify button in the Style dialog box if you want to create new TOC styles for the template you are working in. If you're adventurous enough to get this far, you probably already know how to create a new style. If you don't, *see also* "Applying Styles for Consistent Formatting" in Part III.

If you add a new heading to your document or if you remove one, you can easily get an up-to-date TOC. To do so, right-click anywhere in the TOC and choose Update Field from the shortcut menu. A dialog box asks how to update the TOC. Choose one of these options and click OK:

✦ **Update Page Numbers Only:** Choose this option to put up-to-date page numbers in the TOC. New headings that you added do not appear in the TOC, nor do headings that you deleted get dropped from it. This option is strictly for handling page numbers.

✦ **Update Entire Table:** Choose this option to get a revamped, entirely up-to-date TOC. New headings are added to the TOC, and headings that you deleted are removed.

Each entry in the TOC works like a hyperlink. Click it, and you go directly to a heading your document. Meanwhile, the Web toolbar appears on-screen. Click the Back and Forward buttons to commute between the TOC and the various headings in your document.

Hidden Text and Secret Messages

Besides writing comments to critique a document, you can critique a document with hidden text. (I explain comments at the start of this part.) Hidden text is not printed along with other text unless you tell Word to print it. All you have to do to see hidden text is click the Show/Hide ¶ button.

The fastest way to enter hidden text is to press Ctrl+Shift+H and start typing. You can also choose Format⇨Font and, in the Effects area in the middle of the Font dialog box, click the Hidden check box. You can't see your hidden text unless you click the Show/Hide ¶ button.

Dotted lines appear below hidden text on-screen. This advertising copywriter used hidden text to show the subliminal messages that the advertisement is meant to convey:

Summer's coming on and that means bathing suit time again and you put on weight since last summer, no doubt. Why not come visit us at the Hayes Street Workout Center? You'll meet lots of friendly people i.e., attractive members of the opposite sex. Come on. You've got nothing to lose — nothing but a few pounds, that is.¶

To see hidden text, click the Show/Hide ¶ button, or choose Tools⇨Options, click the View tab, and click the Hidden Text check box in the Formatting Marks area of the dialog box. When it's time to hide the text again, click the Show/Hide ¶ button, or open the Options dialog box and remove the check mark from the Hidden Text check box on the View tab.

If you'd like to print the hidden text in a document, make sure that you won't embarrass yourself by printing it and then choose Tools⇨Options, click the Print tab, and click the Hidden Text check box in the Include with Document part of the dialog box.

Indexing a Document

A good index is a thing of beauty. User manuals, reference works of any length, and reports that readers will refer to all require indexes. Except for the table of contents, the only way to find information in a long document is to look in the index.

An index entry can be formatted in many ways. You can cross-reference index entries, list a page range in an index entry, and break out an index entry into subentries and sub-subentries. To help you with your index, this figure explains indexing terminology:

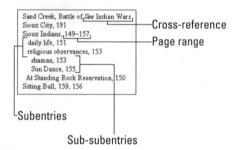

Writing a good index entry is as hard as writing good, descriptive headings. As you enter index entries in your document, ask yourself how you would look up information in the index if you were reading it, and enter your index entries accordingly.

Marking index items in the document

Marking index items yourself is easier than it seems. After you open the Mark Index Entry dialog box, it stays open so that you can scroll through your document and make entries.

1. If you see a word in your document that you can use as a main, top-level entry, select it. You can save a little time that way, as you see shortly. Otherwise, if you don't see a word that you can use, place the cursor in the paragraph or heading whose topic you want to include in the index.

2. Press Alt+Shift+X. The Mark Index Entry dialog box appears. If you selected a word, it appears in the Main Entry box.

3. Choose how you want to handle this index entry. When you enter the text, don't put a comma or period after it. Word does that when it generates the index. The text that you enter will appear in your index.

- **Main entry:** If you're entering a main, top-level entry, leave the text in the Main Entry box (if it's already there), or type new text to describe this entry, or edit the text that's already there. Leave the Subentry box blank.

- **Subentry:** To create a subentry, enter text in the Subentry box. The subentry text will appear in the index below the main entry text, so make sure that there is text in the Main Entry box and that the subentry text fits under the main entry.

- **Sub-subentry:** A sub-subentry is the third level in the hierarchy. To create a sub-subentry, type the subentry in the Subentry box, enter a colon (:), and type the sub-subentry.

4. Decide how to handle the page reference in the entry:

- **Cross-reference:** To go without a page reference and refer the reader to another index entry, click Cross-reference and type the other entry in the text box after the word *See*. What you type here appears in your index, so be sure that the topic you refer the reader to is really in the index.

- **Current Page:** Click this option to enter a single page number after the entry.

- **Page Range:** Click this option if you're indexing a subject that covers several pages in your document. A page range index entry looks something like this: "Sioux Indians, 145–157." To make a page range entry, you must create a bookmark for the range. Click outside the dialog box to get back to your document, and select all the text in the page range. Then choose Insert⇨Bookmark, type a name in the Bookmark Name box (you may as well type the name of the index entry), and click Add. Back in the Mark Index Entry dialog box, click the Page Range option button, click the down arrow, and choose your bookmark from the list. Click Mark when you get to Step 6, not Mark All.

5. You can boldface or italicize a page number or page range by clicking a Page Number Format check box. In some indexes, the page or page range where the topic is explained in the most depth is italicized or boldfaced so that readers can get to the juiciest parts first.

6. If you selected a word in Step 1, you can click Mark All to have Word go through the document and mark all words identical to the one in the Main Entry box. Click Mark to put this single entry in the index.

7. Click outside the Mark Index Entry dialog box and find the next topic or word that you want to mark for the index.

8. Repeat Steps 3 through 7 until you've marked all your index entries, and then click Close to close the Mark Index Entry dialog box.

 A bunch of ugly field codes appear in your document. You can render them invisible by clicking the Show/Hide ¶ button. Now you can go ahead and generate the index.

Generating an index

After you mark the index entries, it's time to generate the index:

1. Place the cursor where you want the index to go, most likely at the end of the document. You might type the word **Index** and format the word in a decorative way.

2. Choose Insert⇨Index and Tables and click the Index tab, if necessary.

3. Choose options in the Index tab of the Index and Tables dialog box. As you do so, watch the Print Preview box to see what happens.

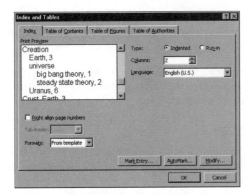

4. When you're done, click OK.

Here are the options on the Index tab of the Index and Tables dialog box:

+ **Type:** Choose Run-in if you want subentries and sub-subentries to run together. Otherwise, stick with the Indented option to indent them.

+ **Columns:** Stick with 2, unless you don't have subentries or sub-subentries and you can squeeze three columns on the page.

+ **Language:** Choose a language for the table if necessary and if you have installed a foreign language dictionary. By doing so, you can run the spell-checker over your index and make sure that the entries are spelled correctly.

+ **Right Align Page Numbers:** Normally, page numbers appear right after entries and are separated from entries by a comma, but you can right-align the entries so they line up under one another with this option.

+ **Tab Leader**: Some index formats (such as Formal) place a *leader* between the entry and the page number. A leader is a series of dots or dashes. If you're working with a format that has a leader, you can choose a leader from the drop-down list.

+ **Formats:** Word offers a number of attractive index layouts. You can choose one from the list.

+ **Modify:** Click this button if you're adventurous and want to create an index style of your own. You must choose From Template in the Formats box in order to do so. In the Style dialog box, choose an Index level style, and then click the Style dialog box's Modify button to get to the Modify Style dialog box and create a style of your own. *See also* "Applying Styles for Consistent Formatting" in Part III if you need help with creating styles.

To update an index after you create or delete entries, right-click the index and then choose Update Field from the shortcut menu, or click the index and press F9.

Editing an index

After you generate an index, read it carefully to make sure that all entries are useful to readers. Inevitably, something doesn't come out right, but you can edit index entries as you would the text in a document. Index field markers are enclosed in angle brackets with the letters *XE* and the text of the index entry in quotation marks, like so: { XE: "Wovoka: Ghost Dance" }. To edit an index marker, click the Show/Hide ¶ button to see the field markers and find the one you need to edit. Then delete letters or type letters as you would do with normal text.

Here's a quick way to find index field markers:

1. Choose Edit⇨Go To or press Ctrl+G.

2. Click Field in the Go to What box.

3. Type **XE** in the Enter Field Name box.

4. Click the Next button until you find the marker you want to edit.

You can also use the Edit⇨Find command to look for index entries. Word finds those as well as text.

Putting Captions on Figures and Tables

Word has a special feature for putting captions on tables, figures, equations, graphs, and a number of other things. Of course, you can add captions yourself, but by letting Word do it, you can compile the captions in tables. At the beginning of a user manual, for example, you can have a table called "Figures in This Manual." Readers can refer to the table when they want to find a figure.

To put a caption on a figure, table, equation, graph, or just about anything else for that matter:

1. Place the cursor where you want the caption to go or select the item for which you want to write a caption.

2. Choose Insert⇨Caption. The Caption dialog box appears.

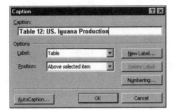

3. In the Label drop-down list, choose which kind of item you're creating a caption for. To create a caption for something that is not on the list, click the New Label button, type a label in the Label box, and click OK.

4. Write a caption in the Caption box. Word supplies the caption label and caption number. You can't change that stuff yourself.

5. If you selected the item before you chose Insert⇨Caption, choose Below Selected Item or Above Selected Item in the Position drop-down list.

6. Click the Numbering button if you want a different numbering scheme than the one shown in the Caption box. In the Caption Numbering dialog box, choose a number scheme from the Format menu and look at the examples at the bottom to see what your choices mean. Click the Include Chapter Number check box and choose a style and separator if you want to include chapter numbers in the numbering scheme. Click OK to get back to the Caption dialog box.

7. Click the AutoCaption button if you want Word to put captions on new tables, equations, or whatever as you create them. The AutoCaption dialog box appears if you make this choice. Click an item in the Add Caption When Inserting box and click OK.

8. Click OK to insert your caption.

See also "Creating a Table of Figures, Graphs, and More," earlier in this part, to see how to compile the captions in a table.

Putting Cross-References in a Document

Cross-references are very handy indeed. They tell readers where to go to find more information on a topic. The problem with cross-references, however, is that the thing being cross-referenced really has to be there. If you send readers to a heading called "The Cat's Pajamas" on page 93 and neither the heading nor the page exists, readers curse and tell you where to go, instead of the other way around.

Fortunately for you, Word lets you know when you make errant cross-references. You can refer readers to headings, page numbers, footnotes, endnotes, and plain old paragraphs. And as long as you create captions for your cross-references with the Insert⇨Caption command, you can also make cross-references to equations, figures, graphs, listings, programs, and tables. If you delete the thing that a cross-reference refers to and render the cross-reference invalid, Word tells you about it the next time you update your cross-references. Best of all, if the page number, numbered item, or text that a cross-reference refers to changes, so does the cross-reference.

To create a cross-reference:

1. Write the first part of the cross-reference text. For example, you could write **To learn more about these cowboys of the pampas, see page** and then enter a blank space. The blank space separates the word *page* from the page number you're about to enter with the Insert⇨Cross-reference command. If you are referring to a heading, write something like **For more information, see "**. Don't enter a blank space this time because the heading text will appear right after the double quotation mark.

2. Choose Insert⇨Cross-reference. The Cross-reference dialog box appears:

3. Choose what type of item you're referring to in the Reference Type menu. If you're referring to a plain old paragraph, choose Bookmark. Then click outside the dialog box, scroll to the paragraph you're referring to, and place a bookmark there (with the Insert⇨Bookmark command).

4. Your choice in the Insert Reference To box determines whether the reference is to text, a page number, or a numbered item. The options in this box are different, depending on what you chose in Step 3. Roughly, your options are these:

- **Text:** Choose this option (Heading Text, Bookmark Text, and so on) to include text in the cross-reference. For example, choose Heading Text if your cross-reference is to a heading.

- **Number:** Choose this option to insert a page number or other kind of number, such as a table number, in the cross-reference.

- **Above/Below:** Choose this option to include the word "above" or "below" to tell readers where, in relation to the cross-reference, the thing being referred to is in your document.

5. If you wish, leave the check mark in the Insert as Hyperlink check box to create a hyperlink as well as a cross-reference. This way, someone reading the document online can click the cross-reference and go directly to what it refers to. (The person can click the Back button on the Web toolbar to return to the cross-reference as well.)

6. To add the word "above" or "below" to the cross-reference, click the Include Above/Below check box. (Whether the check box is available depends on which Reference Type option you chose.) For example, a cross-reference to a page number would say, "See page 9 below."

7. In the For Which box, tell Word 2000 where the thing you're referring to is located. To do so, select a heading, bookmark, footnote, endnote, equation, figure, graph, or whatnot in the menu. In long documents, you will surely have to click the scroll bar to find the one you want.

8. Click Insert.

9. Click the Close button or press Esc.

10. Back in your document, enter the rest of the cross-reference text, if necessary.

When you finish creating your document, update all the cross-references. To do that, press Ctrl+A to select the entire document. Then press F9 or right-click in the document and choose Update Field from the shortcut menu.

If the thing referred to in a cross-reference is no longer in your document , you see `Error! Reference source not found` where the cross-reference should be. To find cross-reference errors in long documents, look for the word *Error!* with the Edit⇨Find command. Investigate what went wrong, and delete the cross-reference or make a new one.

Putting Footnotes and Endnotes in Documents

A *footnote* is a reference, bit of explanation, or comment that appears at the bottom of the page and is referred to by a number or symbol in the text. An *endnote* is the same thing, only it appears at the end of the chapter or document. If you've written a scholarly paper of any kind, you know what a drag footnotes and endnotes are.

Word takes some of the drudgery out of footnotes and endnotes. If you delete or add one, for example, all the others are renumbered. And you don't have to worry about long footnotes because Word adjusts the page layout to make room for them. You can change the numbering scheme of footnotes and endnotes at will. All you have to worry about is entering all those citations correctly.

Inserting a footnote or endnote

To insert a footnote or endnote in a document:

1. Place the cursor in the text where you want the note's symbol or number to appear.

2. Choose Insert⇨Footnote. The Footnote and Endnote dialog box appears.

3. Choose whether you're entering a footnote or endnote in the Insert area of the dialog box.

4. In the Numbering area, click AutoNumber if you want Word to number the notes automatically or Custom Mark to insert a symbol of your own. If you want to insert a symbol, type it in the Custom Mark box, or click the Symbol button and choose one from the Symbol dialog box. If you go this route, you have to enter a symbol each time you insert a note. Not only that, but you may have to enter two or three symbols for the second and third notes on each page or document.

5. Click OK. If you are in Normal view, a notes box opens at the bottom of the screen with the cursor beside the number of the note you're about to enter. In Print Layout view, Word scrolls to the bottom of the page or end of the document or section so that you can enter the note.

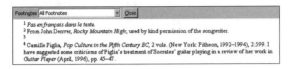

6. Type your footnote or endnote.

7. Click Close when you're done in Normal view; in Print Layout view, click in the middle of the screen to return to the main text.

To read a footnote or endnote, carefully put the pointer on top of its reference number in the text. A yellow box appears with the text of the footnote or endnote.

Changing the numbering scheme and position of notes

Changing the numbering scheme and positioning of endnotes and footnotes is quite easy:

1. Choose Insert⇨Footnote.

2. Click the Options button in the Footnote and Endnote dialog box. The Note Options dialog box appears.

3. Click the All Footnotes or All Endnotes tab. The options on these tabs are nearly the same:

- **Place At:** For footnotes, choose Bottom of Page to put footnotes at the bottom of the page no matter where the text ends; choose Beneath Text to put footnotes directly below the last text line on the page. For endnotes, choose End of

Section if your document is divided into sections (such as chapters) and you want endnotes to appear at the back of sections; choose End of Document to put all endnotes at the very back of the document.

- **Number Format:** Choose A B C, i ii iii, or another numbering scheme. You can also enter symbols by choosing the last option on this drop-down list.

- **Start At:** To start numbering the notes at a place other than 1, A, or i, enter 2, B, ii, or whatever in this box.

- **Numbering:** To number the notes continuously from the start of your document to the end, choose Continuous. Choose Restart Each Section to begin anew at each section of your document. For footnotes, you can begin anew on each page by choosing Restart Each Page.

- **Convert:** This very convenient button is for fickle scholars who suddenly decide that their endnotes should be foot-notes or vice versa. Click it and choose an option in the Convert Notes dialog box to turn footnotes into endnotes, turn endnotes into footnotes, or — in documents with both endnotes and footnotes — make the endnotes footnotes and the footnotes endnotes.

4. Click OK in the Note Options dialog box.

5. Click OK in the Footnote and Endnote dialog box.

Deleting, moving, and editing notes

If a devious editor tells you that a footnote or endnote is in the wrong place, that you don't need a note, or that you need to change the text in a note, all is not lost:

- ✦ **Editing:** To edit a note, double-click its number or symbol in the text. You see the note on-screen. Edit the note at this point.

- ✦ **Moving:** To move a note, select its number or symbol in the text, and drag it to a new location or cut and paste it to a new location.

- ✦ **Deleting:** To delete a note, select its number or symbol and press the Delete key.

Footnotes and endnotes are renumbered when you move or delete them.

Tracking Revisions to Documents

When many hands go into revising a document, figuring out who made revisions to what is impossible. And more importantly, it's impossible to tell what the original, first draft looked like.

To help you keep track of changes to documents, Word offers the Tools➪Track Changes command. When this command is in effect, all changes to the document are recorded in a different color, with one color for each reviser. New text is underlined, a line is drawn through text that has been deleted, and a vertical line appears in the margin to show where changes were made. By moving the pointer over a change, you can read the name of the person who made it. Then you can accept or reject each change. You can also "compare" the first draft of a document with subsequent drafts to see where changes were made.

To give you an idea of what change marks look like, here are the first two lines of Vladimir Nabokov's autobiography *Speak, Memory* with marks to show where he made changes to his first draft.

> Vladimir Nabokov, Tuesday, November 10, 1998 3:53 AM:
> Inserted
>
> The cradle rocks above an abyss, and ~~Vulgar~~ common sense
> ~~assures~~ tells us that our existence is but a brief ~~strip~~
> crack of light between two extremities of ~~complete~~
> darkness. Although the two are identical twins, man, as a
> rule, ~~maybe we~~ views the prenatal abyss one with
> ~~considerably~~ more calm ~~equanimity~~ than the one he ~~is~~ ~~we are~~
> heading for (at some forty-five hundred heart beats an
> hour).

Marking the changes

To keep track of where changes are made to a document, you can either double-click TRK on the status bar, or if you want to be specific about how changes are recorded, you can do the following:

1. Choose Tools➪Track Changes➪Highlight Changes. You see the Highlight Changes dialog box.

2. Click the Track Changes While Editing check box.

3. If you don't want to see the revision marks on-screen, click the Highlight Changes on §creen check box to remove the check mark. Changes to the document are recorded with this option, but they aren't shown. In a document with a lot of revisions, choose this option to work without all that clutter on-screen.

4. Click the Highlight Changes in Printed Document check box if you want change marks to appear on your document when you print it.

5. Click OK.

Now you can start to make changes. If you are the first author to have a crack at this document, your changes appear in blue. If you are the second author, they appear in magenta. Word can tell when a new reviser has gotten hold of a document and assigns a new color accordingly.

To choose a revision color of your own and otherwise tell Word how to mark changes, choose Tools⇨ Track Changes⇨Highlight Changes and click the Options button in the Highlight Changes dialog box, or choose Tools⇨Options and click the Track Changes tab in the Options dialog box. Then, with the drop-down lists on the Track Changes tab, tell Word how to mark inserted text, deleted text, and changes to formatting and where to put the line in the margin that shows where changes were made. Be sure to watch the Preview boxes to see what your choices amount to.

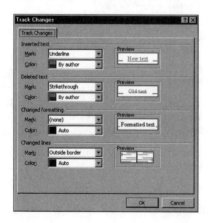

Comparing and merging documents

The fastest way to track revisions may be to pass out copies, tell others to make changes, and then "compare" or "merge" the revised document with the original. To compare or merge documents, use the following commands:

+ **Tools⇨Track Changes⇨Compare Documents:** Choose this command if you are working on a copy of the original document. In the Select File to Compare with Current Document dialog box, find the original file, select it, and choose Open. Marks appear to show where you made changes to the original document.

+ **Tools⇨Merge Documents:** Choose this command if you have the original document and want to see what others have done to it. In the Select File to Merge Into Current Document dialog box, click the revised version of the file and click Open. Marks show where others made changes to your original document.

Accepting and rejecting revisions

Now that the changes have been made, you can decide what to do about them. Word offers two means of reviewing changes to a document, the Reviewing toolbar and the Accept or Reject Changes dialog box. To review changes one at a time:

1. Choose Tools⇨Track Changes⇨Accept or Reject Changes, or right-click on a toolbar and choose Reviewing from the shortcut menu.

Who made the change

2. To start searching for change marks, click a Find button in the dialog box or click the Previous Change or Next Change button on the toolbar. Word highlights a change on-screen. In the dialog box, the name of the person who made the revision appears in the Changes box.

3. In the dialog box, click Accept to keep the change or Reject to reverse it. If you're working with the toolbar, click the Accept Change or Reject Change button.

4. Word finds the next change. Either reject or accept it.

5. To help make sense of what you're doing, you can choose a View option in the dialog box:

• Changes with Highlighting shows revision marks on-screen.

• Changes without Highlighting shows the changes without the revision marks so that you can see what changes will look like if you accept them.

- <u>O</u>riginal shows what the document looked like before any changes were made so that you can see what happens to the document if you reject a change.

6. Keep accepting or rejecting. If you change your mind about a revision, click the <u>U</u>ndo button.

7. Click Close or press Esc when you're done.

If you trust your colleagues and have total faith in their revisions, you can accept their revisions in one fell swoop. Click the Accept All button in the Accept or Reject Changes dialog box. When Word asks whether you really want to accept them all, click Yes. You can reject all the revisions just as easily by choosing Reject All.

Potpourri

On the *Jeopardy!* TV show, the last column on the question board is sometimes called "Potpourri." That's where they put oddball questions that can't fit in any category. Part VIII is called "Potpourri," too, because the topics covered here don't fit in the other seven parts of the book.

Some of the tasks in this part are absolutely essential; others are downright wacky. But maybe I'm being "judgmental," as we say in California, and all this stuff is actually very useful. I should let you be the judge of what is and what isn't useful in Part VIII.

In this part . . .

- ✔ Backing up files so that you have copies in case of an emergency
- ✔ Finding a lost file
- ✔ Checking out a document's properties
- ✔ Highlighting important text in a document
- ✔ Importing files from, and exporting files to, other word processors
- ✔ Adding special effects to your document
- ✔ Protecting your files with passwords

Backing Up Your Work

If an elephant steps on your computer or your computer breaks down and can't be repaired, you lose all the files you worked so hard to create. You have to start from scratch and create your files all over again, unless you backed them up. *Backing up* means to make a copy of a file and put it on a floppy disk, zip disk, or other place from which you can retrieve files in the event of a fire, pestilence, coffee spill, computer breakdown, or other emergency.

Besides backing up files to a floppy disk or zip disk, you can back up files in special directories on your hard disk. The disadvantage of backing up this way, however, is that the files are still on your computer. If your computer breaks down altogether, you can't get your files back. However, you can recover them if there is a power failure or other untoward event that doesn't damage your computer.

Backing up to an external location

To back up a file to a location outside your computer, such as a floppy disk or zip disk, you leave Word and do the job with Windows:

1. Close the file if it is open.

2. Open the Windows Explorer utility. To do this, click the Start button and choose Programs⇨Windows Explorer. The Windows Explorer window appears on-screen.

3. Find the folder with the file you want to back up. To do so, click plus signs next to the folder names on the left side of the screen to see subfolders, if necessary, and then select the folder with the file you want to back up. The file appears on the right side of the Windows Explorer screen.

4. When you see the file that you're backing up, click and drag it to the place where you will store the backup copy. To store it on a floppy disk, for example, drag it to the Floppy icon at the top of the Folders window pane and release the mouse button.

The Copying message box appears. It tells you that the file is being copied, and it shows a picture of pieces of paper being flung from one folder to another.

Now you can get the file back by copying it from the floppy disk or zip disk to your computer. Be sure to save your floppy disk or zip disk in a safe place away from your computer. A fire, for example, would destroy your computer and your backup files if you keep your backups on the desk next to your computer.

Backing up files in Word

If you accidentally unplug the computer, a power failure occurs, or your computer hangs while you are working on a document, you can recover your document as long as you have told Word to make AutoRecover files and backup copies of the documents on your computer. Follow these steps to tell Word to back up your files in the event of a power failure or computer hang:

1. Choose Tools⇨Options.

2. Click the Save tab of the Options dialog box.

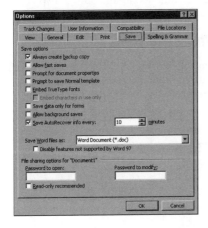

3. Click the Always Create Backup Copy check box.

4. Click the Save AutoRecover Info Every check box and enter a number in the Minutes box to tell Word how often to make a document recovery file. Word uses these files to restore documents that were on-screen when the computer died.

5. Click OK.

After you choose the Always Create Backup Copy and Save AutoRecover Info Every options, you can get copies of files after a power failure. So why would you choose one option over the other, or both options? Here's why:

✦ **Save AutoRecover Info Every:** With this option, Word makes a document recovery copy of your file every few minutes (depending on what you enter in the Minutes box). After a power failure occurs and you start Word again, the application opens the AutoRecover files of the documents that were on-screen when the computer died. These documents aren't entirely up to date, but they are good as of the last time Word made the document recovery file.

✦ **Always Create Backup Copy:** With this option, Word makes a second copy of your file and keeps it in the same folder as the original. However, the backup copy is made only when you, and not Word, save the file. If a power failure occurs, you can't recover the work you did in the last few minutes, although you can recover the version of the file that was saved the last time *you* saved the file.

Backup copies made with the Always Create Backup Copy option eat up a lot of disk space. If you choose this option, two copies of everything you do in Word are stored on disk. That takes up a lot of room.

Recovering a file after a power failure

Suppose that a power failure occurs. You can recover a file from its AutoRecover cousin by following these steps as long as you checked the Save AutoRecover Info Every check box:

1. Start Word. All the documents that you were working on when lightning struck are opened on-screen. You see *(Recovered)* after their names.

2. Choose File⇨Save As.

3. Click the Save button in the Save As dialog box.

4. Click Yes when Word asks whether you want to replace the existing document.

The work that you did in the last few minutes is lost, but the work that was complete the last time Word made an AutoRecover copy of the file is restored.

Opening a backup copy of a file

To get the backup copy of a file after a power failure or other electrical accident:

1. Click the Open button, press Ctrl+O, or choose File⇨Open to display the Open dialog box.

2. Go to the folder where the original file was stored and click it.

3. Click the down arrow on the Files of Type box at the bottom of the dialog box and choose All Files.

4. Look for the backup copy and click it. Backup copy names start with the words *Backup of* and end with the *.wbk* extension. If you have trouble finding a backup copy of a file, click the down arrow beside the Views button, choose Details from the drop-down list, and look for the words "Microsoft Word Backup Document" in the Type column next to the filenames.

5. Click <u>O</u>pen.

Finding a Missing File

Occasionally, you forget the name of a file you want to open. Or you remember the name but forget the name of the folder you put the file in. When that happens, you can search for the file with options in the Open dialog box:

1. Click the Open button, press Ctrl+O, or choose <u>F</u>ile⇨<u>O</u>pen to get to the Open dialog box.

2. If you can remember roughly where you stored the file, use the Look <u>I</u>n drop-down list, Up One Level button, and other tools in the Open dialog box to find the folder in which it is located. If you have no idea where the file is located on your computer, don't worry about it. Your search will take longer, that's all.

3. Click the Too<u>l</u>s button and choose <u>F</u>ind from the drop-down list. You see the Find dialog box.

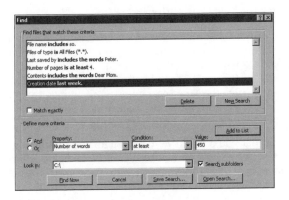

4. In the <u>P</u>roperty drop-down list, select an aspect of the file that you know something about. Choose File Name, for example, if you remember all or part of the name of the file you are looking for; choose Last Modified if you know roughly when you last saved the file.

5. From the <u>C</u>ondition drop-down list, choose an option that helps describe the file. The options on this menu vary depending on the choice you made in the <u>P</u>roperty drop-down list.

6. In the Val<u>u</u>e text box, enter a value or handful of characters to further describe the file. What you enter in this box also depends on which aspect of the file you are trying to describe.

7. Click the <u>A</u>dd to List button. The search criteria you just created are listed in the Find Files <u>T</u>hat Match These Criteria box at the top of the Find dialog box.

8. Repeat Steps 4 through 7 to describe more aspects of the file. The more you can tell Word about the file, the better your chances of finding it.

9. Click the Searc<u>h</u> Subfolders check box, if it isn't already checked off, to search in the subfolders of the folder or drive that is listed in the Look <u>I</u>n box.

10. Click the Match E<u>x</u>actly check box if you included text criteria — filenames, author names, and so on — in your search and you want Word to look only for words whose upper and lowercase letters are identical to those in the Find Files <u>T</u>hat Match These Criteria box.

11. In the Look <u>I</u>n drop-down list, choose which drive or which part of your computer to search. (Your best bet probably is to choose drive C to search the hard disk.) If you completed Step 2, the name of the folder in which you want to search already appears in the Look <u>I</u>n box.

12. Click the <u>F</u>ind Now button.

If Word can find the file you are looking for, its name appears in the Open dialog box. Click the file's name and click the Open button to open your file. If Word can't find the file, try, try, try again. Click the Too<u>l</u>s button and choose Find to return to the Find dialog box. Then either click the New Search button to change the terms of the search or click a criterion or two on the Find Files That Match These Criteria list and click the Delete button to remove those criteria.

Suppose that you often have to search for the same stray file. In that case, describe the file in the Find dialog box, click the Save Search button, enter a descriptive name in the Save Search dialog box, and click OK. Next time you want to search for the file, don't bother formulating the search criteria. Instead, click the Open Search button, choose a name in the Open Search dialog box, and click the Open button to describe your stray file in the Find dialog box.

Getting Information about a Document

Word keeps information about your documents. You can find out how long you've worked on a document, how many times you've saved it, when you created it, and how many words it contains, among other things. You can also enter words to help Word find your document if it is lost.

The fast way to get the statistics on a document is to choose Tools⇨Word Count. A dialog box appears with the number of words, characters, pages, paragraphs, and lines.

To get detailed stats on a document:

1. Choose File⇨Properties. A dialog box titled [Name of Document] Properties appears.

2. Click the tabs to review or make changes.

3. Click OK.

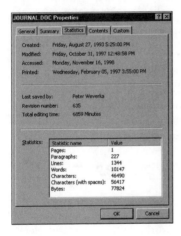

The Statistics tab tells when the document was created, when and who last saved it, and how much work went into it in terms of time, pages, words, and characters, among other things.

The Summary tab lists the author, title, and other pertinent information. If you think that you may lose your file someday, enter words in the Category and Keywords boxes to help find the file.

The General tab tells you how long the file is and whether it's an archive, read-only, hidden, or system file.

The Contents tab lists the headings to which you applied heading styles. To see the headings, click the Save Preview Picture check box on the Summary tab.

The Custom tab lets you create other means of keeping statistics on your documents.

Highlighting Parts of a Document

One way to call attention to the most important parts of a document is to highlight them. You can do that very easily with the Highlight button on the Formatting toolbar:

1. Scroll to the part of the document that you want to highlight.

2. Click the Highlight button. The cursor changes into a fat pencil.

3. Drag the cursor over the text you want to highlight.

4. Click the Highlight button again when you're done.

To choose a color for highlighting, click the down arrow beside the Highlight button and then click a color on the color menu.

Highlight marks are printed along with the text. To get rid of them, follow these steps:

1. Select the document or the text from which you want to remove the highlights.

2. Click the down arrow to open the Highlight color menu.

3. Click None.

Importing and Exporting Files

Word makes it easy to use files from other Microsoft Office applications, from other versions of Microsoft Word (including Macintosh versions), from Write and Works, and from WordPerfect. Other files are a different story. For example, Word is not on speaking terms with WordPro, not to mention antique word processors like WordStar, XYWrite, and MultiMate (oh, the memories!).

It is easy to export files to, and import files from, applications that Word recognizes and is friendly with. Your coworkers who have WordPerfect, for example, can use your files, but your friends who have other word processors may well have to use stripped-down versions of your files with the text but none of the formats.

Even when you import or export a file successfully, some things get lost. For example, special characters and symbols often don't translate well. Nor do certain fonts. Carefully proofread files that you've imported or exported to make sure that everything came out right.

Importing a file

To import a file, you open it and let Word turn it into a Word file:

1. Click the Open button, press Ctrl+O, or choose File➪Open to display the Open dialog box.

2. Find the file you want to import in the Open dialog box and click it.

3. Click the down arrow in the Files of Type box and see whether the kind of file you want to import is on the list. If it is, click it. If it isn't, try choosing Rich Text Format. This format strives to retain all the formatting of non-Word documents. If worse comes to worse, you can always click the Text Files option. With this option, Word strips all formats such as boldfacing and fonts from the file, but at least you get to keep the text.

4. Click Open.

Here's one way to get around file-importing impasses: If the application that you want to import the file from works in Windows, open the application, open the file you want to copy, and copy the parts of the file you need to the Clipboard. Then paste what is on the Clipboard into Word.

Another way to get around the problem of not being able to import a file is to see whether the other application can save files in Microsoft Word format. If it can, save the file as a Microsoft Word file in the other application and then open it in Word.

Word 2000 files can be opened in Word 97, the predecessor to Word 2000. However, to save a Word 2000 file so that a friend or coworker who has Word 95 or Word 6 can use it, choose File➪ Save As, open the Save As Type menu in the Save As dialog box, and choose Word 6.0/95 from the list.

Exporting a file

To export a file so that someone with another kind of word processor can use it, you save the file in a new format:

1. Choose File➪Save As.

2. Find the file you want to export in the Save As dialog box and click it.

3. Click the down arrow in the Save as Type menu and see whether the kind of file you want to export is on the list. If it is on the list, choose it. If it isn't, choose either Rich Text Format or Text Only with Line Breaks:

- Rich Text Format retains the formatting of the text, but some word processors can't understand it.

- In case worse comes to worse, Text Only with Line Breaks strips out all the formatting but retains the text and line breaks.

4. Click <u>S</u>ave.

Including Video Clips, Animation, and Sound in Documents

Yes, it can be done. Including a video sequence or sound file in a Word document is possible as long as your computer has speakers, a sound card, and the ability to play video. Follow these steps to turn a plain-Jane document into a miniature drive-in movie theater:

1. Open Windows Explorer or My Computer to the folder where the sound file or video clip you want to include in your Word document is located. (Windows Explorer and My Computer are programs that come with Windows.)

2. Open the Word document that you want to put the sound file or video clip inside.

3. Drag the sound file or video clip into the Word document. A speaker icon or mini-video screen appears.

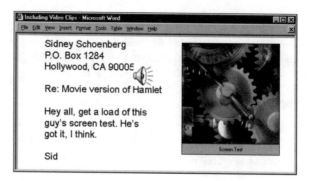

4. Drag the speaker icon or mini-video screen where you want it to appear on the page. ***See also*** "Handling Objects on Pages" in Part VI to find out how to move and change the size of objects such as the speaker icon and mini-video screen.

To hear a sound file or play a video clip in a Word document, double-click it.

Including a video clip in a Word document makes the document grow in size to enormous proportions. As little as three seconds of video without sound adds about 1 megabyte to the size of a file!

Rather than include a video clip, maybe you should "animate" a few words to make your document livelier. Select the words, choose Format⇨Font, click the Text Effects tab in the Font dialog box, make a choice from the Animations list (the Preview box shows precisely what you are choosing), and click OK. The (none) option in the Animations list is for removing text animations. The animations require far less disk space than video clips do.

Protecting Your Work with Passwords

To keep jealous coworkers, your spouse, your boss, and unauthorized biographers from opening a file, you can protect it with a password. You can also allow others to view a document but not make changes to it unless they have the password. You can even protect a part of a document to keep others from changing it.

Keeping others from opening a file

To keep others from opening a document unless they have the password:

1. Open the document.

2. Choose Tools⇨Options and click the Save tab in the Options dialog box.

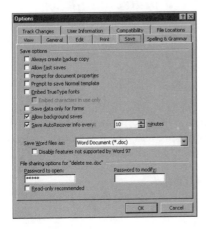

3. Type your password in the Password to Open box. Instead of letters, asterisks appear in the box in case a spy is looking over your shoulder. (That spy, however, could watch your fingers to see which letters you type.) Passwords can be 15 characters long. If you include upper and lowercase letters in your password, remember them well because you have to reproduce your password exactly whenever you open this file.

4. Click OK.

5. In the Confirm Password dialog box, type the password again. If you don't enter it correctly, Word tells you so and sends you back to the Options dialog box.

6. Click OK in the Confirm Password dialog box.

After you attach a password to a document, you have to save the document to make the password go into effect.

It almost goes without saying, but you must never, never forget your password. If you forget it, you simply cannot open the file again!

Everybody has different advice for choosing a password that isn't likely to be forgotten or discovered, and everybody agrees that you shouldn't use your name or the names of family members or pets, because miscreants try those names first when they try to crack open a file. Here's a good tip for choosing passwords: Pick your favorite foreign city and spell it backwards. My favorite foreign city is in Greece. If I needed a password, it would be **ufroC**.

Opening a password-protected file

To open a file that has been given a password:

1. Open the file as you normally would. The Password dialog box appears.

2. Type the password and click OK.

If Word tells you that it can't open the file because you've given the wrong password, you may have entered the password with the wrong combination of upper and lowercase characters. Try again, using different capital and lowercase letters.

Removing a password

To remove a password, all you have to do is this:

1. Open the file.

2. Choose Tools➪Options.

3. Click the Save tab.

4. Delete the asterisks from the Password to Open box.

5. Click OK.

Keeping others from changing a file

Besides keeping others from looking at a file, you can keep them from making changes to a file unless they have the password. This way, others can open the file, but they must have the password in order to edit it.

1. Open the document.

2. Choose Tools⇨Options and click the Save tab in the Options dialog box.

3. Type your password in the Password to Modify box. The usual asterisks appear as you type the password.

4. Click OK.

5. In the Confirm Password dialog box, type the password again.

6. Click OK.

Whenever anyone tries to open this file, he or she sees this dialog box:

By entering the correct password and clicking OK, the other user can view and make changes to the file. If the other user doesn't have the password, he or she can still view and make changes to the file by clicking the Read Only button. However, when the other user tries to save the file, he or she will have to save it, along with the changes made to it, under a different filename.

Protecting parts of a document from changes

With Word's Tools⇨Protect Document command, you can prevent others from making changes in various ways. You can keep users who don't have the password from changing annotations and forms, and you can also force all changes made to the document to be recorded with revision marks. Here's how:

1. Open the document that you want to protect.

2. Choose <u>T</u>ools➪<u>P</u>rotect Document. The Protect Document dialog box appears.

3. In the Protect Document For area, choose how you want to protect the file:

- **<u>T</u>racked Changes:** All changes made to the document are recorded with revision marks. This way, you always know where changes were made.

- **<u>C</u>omments:** Reviewers can make their own comments but can't change the comments that are there already.

- **<u>F</u>orms:** Users can fill in form fields, but they can't change the text of the form.

4. If you want to protect the forms in only one or two sections in a document, make sure that the <u>F</u>orms option button is selected, click the <u>S</u>ections button, and click to remove the check marks from the sections that you *don't* want to protect. Then click OK.

5. Enter a password in the <u>P</u>assword box. Passwords can be 15 characters long. Remember this password and the exact combination of uppercase and lowercase letters because you and other users need to type it the same way when you want to make changes to comments or forms or make changes without the revision marks showing.

6. Click OK to close the Protect Document dialog box.

Now users have to enter the correct password to change existing comments or forms or to track changes without revision marks.

To "unprotect" a document so that users can make changes at will, choose <u>T</u>ools➪Un<u>p</u>rotect Document.

Techie Talk

AutoCorrect: Word "autocorrects" what it thinks are errors in documents. Certain words are autocorrected, as are capitalization errors.

browser: A computer program that connects to Web sites and displays Web pages. The most popular browsers are Internet Explorer and Netscape Navigator.

cell: The box that is formed in a table where a row and column intersect. Each cell holds one data item.

check box: A square box inside a dialog box. Click an option's check box to place a check mark in the box and activate the option. Click again to remove the check mark and render the option dormant.

click: To press the left mouse button once. Not to be confused with *clique*, a like-minded assortment of high school students who dress and talk the same way. *See also* right-click.

clip art: Graphics and pictures that can be imported into a computer file.

Clipboard: A holding tank to which you can copy or move text and graphics. Text and graphics can be pasted from the Clipboard into a document.

crop: To cut off part of a graphic.

Ctrl+click: To click the left mouse button while holding down the Ctrl key. Ctrl+click to select more than one item in a dialog box. *See also* Shift+click.

curb feeler: A flexible metal rod that was attached to the right rear bumper of most pre-1955 cars. Curb feelers helped with parallel parking, as drivers heard a scraping noise when their cars came too close to the curb.

cursor: An on-screen symbol that tells you what the computer is doing. Cursors include the insertion point (the vertical line that blinks on and off and tells you where text goes when you press the keys) and the mouse cursor, which looks like an arrow when you move the mouse over something you can choose or like a large egotistical *I* when it's in a document window. Also someone who curses at a computer screen.

default: Options that are already selected when you open a dialog box are known as default options. Default options are the ones that users of a program are most likely to choose on their own.

dialog box: A box that appears on-screen when Word needs more information to complete a task. *See also* check box, drop-down list, option button, radio button.

document: A letter, report, announcement, or proclamation that you create with Word. Any file you create with Word is considered a document.

double-click: To click twice with the left mouse button.

drag and drop: The fastest way to copy or move text or clip art from one place to another. Select the text, hold down the left mouse button, drag the text to a new location, and release the mouse button.

drop cap: An ornamental first letter, larger than the other letters, that drops three or four lines into the text and appears at the start of articles and chapters.

drop-down list: A menu box with a down arrow at its side. Click the down arrow, and a menu appears with options you can choose.

field: A code in a file that represents information that varies. For example, if you put a "today's date" field at the top of a letter you write on July 31, 2000, but print the letter on August 5, 2000, the letter is dated August 5, 2000. Also a flat place where soccer is played or crops are grown.

file extension: The three-character extension following the period in filenames. Word files have the *.doc* (document) extension. Each type of computer file has its own three-letter file extension.

font: A distinctive typeface design. Fonts are found on the Font menu on the Formatting toolbar.

footer: A line at the bottom of each page of a document that usually includes the document's name, a page number, or similar information. *See also* header.

function keys: The ten or twelve F keys along the top of the keyboard. Function keys are used to give commands.

gridlines: The gray lines that show where columns and rows are in a table. Choose Table⇨Show Gridlines or Table⇨Hide Gridlines to see or display the gridlines.

gutter: In a bound document, the part of the paper that the binding eats into. Also, in a newspaper-style document, the space between columns.

hanging indent: An indent in which the second and subsequent lines in a paragraph are indented farther from the left margin than the first line. When you create numbered and bulleted lists in Word by clicking the Numbering or Bullets button, you create a hanging indent.

header: A line at the top of the pages of a document that usually lists the document's name, the page number, or similar information. *See also* footer.

header row: The labels along the top row or rows of a table or database that explain what is in the columns below.

hot key: The underlined letter in a command name. Press the hot key or Alt+ the hot key to execute a command quickly. Also called a *shortcut key.*

hyperlink: A link between two Web pages or two different places in the same Web page. Click a hyperlink and you go directly to another Web page or another place on the same Web page.

kerning: To make a pair of letters farther apart or closer together.

leading: The vertical distance between two lines of type.

margin: The empty space on a page between the text and the top, bottom, left, and right borders of the page. Text is indented from the margin, not the side of the page.

mouse: The soap-shaped thing on your desk that you roll to make the mouse cursor move on-screen. If you reach for your mouse and feel fur or hear a squeaking sound, you should stop eating at your desk. The mouse has a left and right button. *See also* click, cursor, right-click.

object: Clip art images, text boxes, shapes, lines, autoshapes, and WordArt images are all objects. The techniques for manipulating objects — for moving and resizing them, for example — are the same.

option button: A button in a dialog box that you click to alter the way in which a command is applied.

orphan: A single line of text at the start of a paragraph that appears at the very bottom of a page. Orphans sort of cheat the reader, because the reader can't tell how long the paragraph is until he or she turns the page. *See also* widow.

paste: To copy text or a graphic from the Clipboard to a document.

point: A unit for measuring the height of type. One point equals $1/72$ of an inch.

radio button: One of a set of two or more option buttons, only one of which can be selected. Radio buttons are round.

right-click: To click with the right mouse button.

save: To copy the data on-screen to the computer's hard disk, a floppy disk, or a network drive. Data is not stored permanently until it has been saved.

scroll: To move through a document or menu by using the scroll bars along the right side or, in the case of wide documents, by using the scroll bar at the bottom of the screen as well.

section: A part of a document. You cannot change page numbering schemes or margin sizes without creating a new section.

Shift+click: To click the left mouse button while holding down the Shift key. Shift+click to select a group of items in a dialog box. *See also* Ctrl+click.

shortcut menu: A menu that appears when you right-click on-screen. Which shortcut menu appears depends on which part of the screen you click.

sort: To arrange the data in a table in a new way.

style: A format for headings, paragraphs, and other parts of a document, as well as characters. You can assign a new style by choosing one from the Style menu on the Formatting toolbar. Never to be confused with the term as it is used to describe a unique way of dressing.

submenu: A short menu that appears when you click a menu command whose name is followed by an arrow.

taskbar: The bar along the bottom of the screen in Windows. The names of computer applications that are running appear on buttons on the taskbar, as do the names of all open Word documents. Click a button to switch to another application or Word document.

template: A collection of styles you can choose from for formatting documents. All the styles in a template appear in the Style menu on the Formatting toolbar. *See also* style.

toolbar: An assortment of buttons for performing tasks.

typewriter: A device used by the ancient Egyptians for imprinting letters on papyrus leaves. According to some archeologists, the typewriter is the forerunner of the word processor.

watermark: A pale decorative image that appears behind the text in the same position on each page.

widow: A very short line, usually one word, that appears at the end of a paragraph. Widows create a lot of ugly white space across the page. *See also* orphan.

Index

Dummies Books™
Bestsellers on Every Topic!

TECHNOLOGY TITLES

...NET

...a Online® For Dummies®, 5th Edition	John Kaufeld	0-7645-0502-5	$19.99 US/$26.99 CAN
...logy Online For Dummies®	Matthew L. Helm & April Leah Helm	0-7645-0377-4	$24.99 US/$35.99 CAN
...et Directory For Dummies®, 2nd Edition	Brad Hill	0-7645-0436-3	$24.99 US/$35.99 CAN
...ternet For Dummies®, 6th Edition	John R. Levine, Carol Baroudi, & Margaret Levine Young	0-7645-0506-8	$19.99 US/$28.99 CAN
...ng Online For Dummies®, 2nd Edition	Kathleen Sindell, Ph.D.	0-7645-0509-2	$24.99 US/$35.99 CAN

...ATING SYSTEMS

...or Dummies®, 3rd Edition	Dan Gookin	0-7645-0361-8	$19.99 US/$28.99 CAN
...® For Dummies®, 2nd Edition	John Hall & Craig Witherspoon	0-7645-0421-5	$24.99 US/$35.99 CAN
...For Dummies®, 4th Edition	John R. Levine & Margaret Levine Young	0-7645-0419-3	$19.99 US/$28.99 CAN
...ws® 98 For Dummies®	Andy Rathbone	0-7645-0261-1	$19.99 US/$28.99 CAN

...NERAL COMPUTING

...g a Computer For Dummies®	Dan Gookin	0-7645-0313-8	$19.99 US/$28.99 CAN
...ms For Dummies®, 3rd Edition	Tina Rathbone	0-7645-0069-4	$19.99 US/$26.99 CAN
...Business Computing For Dummies®	Brian Underdahl	0-7645-0287-5	$24.99 US/$35.99 CAN
...ding & Fixing PCs For Dummies®, 4th Edition	Andy Rathbone	0-7645-0418-5	$19.99 US/$28.99 CAN

...S

...soft® Office 2000 For Windows® ...r Dummies®	Wallace Wang & Roger C. Parker	0-7645-0452-5	$19.99 US/$28.99 CAN
...soft® Office 2000 For Windows® ...r Dummies®, Quick Reference	Doug Lowe & Bjoern Hartsfvang	0-7645-0453-3	$12.99 US/$19.99 CAN
...soft® Office 98 For Macs® For Dummies®	Tom Negrino	0-7645-0229-8	$19.99 US/$28.99 CAN

...BASE

...ss 2000 For Windows® For Dummies®	John Kaufeld	0-7645-0444-4	$19.99 US/$28.99 CAN
...ss 97 For Windows® For Dummies®	John Kaufeld	0-7645-0048-1	$19.99 US/$26.99 CAN
...al Reports 7 For Dummies®	Douglas J. Wolf	0-7645-0548-3	$24.99 US/$34.99 CAN
...Warehousing For Dummies®	Alan R. Simon	0-7645-0170-4	$24.99 US/$34.99 CAN
...net & Web Databases For Dummies®	Paul Litwin	0-7645-0221-2	$29.99 US/$42.99 CAN

GENERAL INTEREST TITLES

...D & BEVERAGE/ENTERTAINING

...rmet Cooking For Dummies®	Charlie Trotter	0-7645-5029-2	$19.99 US/$26.99 CAN
...ing For Dummies®	Marie Rama & John Mariani	0-7645-5076-4	$19.99 US/$26.99 CAN
...an Cooking For Dummies®	Cesare Casella & Jack Bishop	0-7645-5098-5	$19.99 US/$26.99 CAN
...e For Dummies®, 2nd Edition	Ed McCarthy & Mary Ewing-Mulligan	0-7645-5114-0	$19.99 US/$26.99 CAN

...RTS

...eball For Dummies®	Joe Morgan with Richard Lally	0-7645-5085-3	$19.99 US/$26.99 CAN
...tball For Dummies®	Howie Long with John Czarnecki	0-7645-5054-3	$19.99 US/$26.99 CAN
...key For Dummies®	John Davidson with John Steinbreder	0-7645-5045-4	$19.99 US/$26.99 CAN

...ME & GARDEN

...cks & Patios For Dummies®	Robert J. Beckstrom & National Gardening Association	0-7645-5075-6	$16.99 US/$24.99 CAN
...wering Bulbs For Dummies®	Judy Glattstein & National Gardening Association	0-7645-5103-5	$16.99 US/$24.99 CAN
...me Improvement For Dummies®	Gene & Katie Hamilton & the Editors of HouseNet, Inc.	0-7645-5005-5	$19.99 US/$26.99 CAN
...wn Care For Dummies®	Lance Walheim & National Gardening Association	0-7645-5077-2	$16.99 US/$24.99 CAN

...REERS

...ver Letters For Dummies®	Joyce Lain Kennedy	1-56884-395-X	$12.99 US/$17.99 CAN
...ol Careers For Dummies®	Marty Nemko, Paul Edwards, & Sarah Edwards	0-7645-5095-0	$16.99 US/$24.99 CAN
...b Interviews For Dummies®	Joyce Lain Kennedy	1-56884-859-5	$12.99 US/$17.99 CAN
...sumes For Dummies®, 2nd Edition	Joyce Lain Kennedy	0-7645-5113-2	$12.99 US/$17.99 CAN

Hungry Minds™

For more information, or to order, call (800)762-2974

FOR DUMMIES™
BESTSELLING BOOK SERIES

Dummies Books™
Bestsellers on Every Topic!

FOR DUMMIES
BOOK REGISTRATION

We want to hear from you!

Visit **dummies.com** to register this book and tell us how you liked it!

- ✔ Get entered in our monthly prize giveaway.

- ✔ Give us feedback about this book — tell us what you like best, what you like least, or maybe what you'd like to ask the author and us to change!

- ✔ Let us know any other *For Dummies* topics that interest you.

Your feedback helps us determine what books to publish, tells us what coverage to add as we revise our books, and lets us know whether we're meeting your needs as a *For Dummies* reader. You're our most valuable resource, and what you have to say is important to us!

Not on the Web yet? It's easy to get started with *Dummies 101: The Internet For Windows 98* or *The Internet For Dummies* at local retailers everywhere.

Or let us know what you think by sending us a letter at the following address:

For Dummies Book Registration
Dummies Press
10475 Crosspoint Blvd.
Indianapolis, IN 46256

BESTSELLING
BOOK SERIES